PADDLING HOME

A Journey Back to Self

ROBYN SINGH

ISBN: 0985590912
ISBN 13: 9780985590918

*This book is dedicated to my family(s), my
paddling ohana the Wa'a (canoe)
and the oceans that connect us all.*

Contents

CONTENTS

Emotion - energy in motion

As Humans, we have two types of memory-

1. Explicit Memory - where there is recall from the brain, and

2. Implicit Memory - where there is only emotional memory and no recall.

Before 18 months of age, the brain structure for recall memory is not even formed, so any emotional experience is stored in the brain as nerve circuits, ready to fire without specific recall.

People who are adopted, especially from birth, have a distinct sense of rejection. It's not unique to all, but it can be particularly strong in them. They can't recall the adoption. They can't recall the separation from the birth mother because theres nothing to recall with, but the emotional memory of separation is deeply imbedded in the nerve circuitry of the brain.

I know for myself, the perception of rejection played havoc with my nerve circuits on a few occasions. When something so seemingly simple happened, my emotional response was really strong and intense and I could never understand why.

It provided enough stimulus for me to be on this path today. I wanted to know all about me, how I tick, who I am and where I came from, and what's wonderful is that it is in the seeking of this knowledge that we learn and view from new perspectives. Then our "exist-dance" starts making sense.

CHAPTER 1

Humble Beginnings

I was told that I was adopted at a very young age. My parents Bob and Kaye would always be my Mum and Dad and I guess it was their duty to inform me.

I was neither upset nor surprised. It felt perfectly normal to me as a six year old and was no big deal. I was happy and blessed with my parents, and life went ahead.

After a long process and much paper work, they picked me up from Brisbane Hospital. I was a bouncing bald headed bundle of joy waiting to start life in Australia.

My Mum and Dad were so happy to meet me. They brought me to my new home at Mermaid Beach. The house where I grew up was about 100 meters from the beach and was right next door to the auction rooms, which my Dad owned. My mum worked with him, running a busy and vibrant used furniture mart. I spent much time there in my early years.

My Mum Kaye was from German descent and grew up in Stanthorpe, one of the only places that get snow in Queensland, her town famous for apples and stone fruit. She grew up in the country with four brothers, and then at young age her family moved to Palm Beach on the Gold Coast. She was a good at sport and played basketball, an enthusiastic scholar, with home economics being a subject she excelled in.

My Mum also taught Sunday School well before I came along. She was an excellent book keeper and had the neatest writing you would ever see.

She met my father in Palm Beach. My Dad ran a fruit market in Currumbin just down the road. She ended up working there for him in the early days and really was by his side through decades of change, a busy life and right until his death. She was truly devoted to him. They married the year before I came into the picture.

My Dad was from a Sikh lineage. Both his parents came from India on a boat and settled in the Tweed area. He was born in Tweed Heads and had a challenging and difficult upbringing. His mother died while giving birth to his brother and this was all before he had turned two. A tough entry into the world. His Dad, was from the Punjab region in the north of India, God bless him. From my Dads stories, he was a hard man, times were tough, and if people knew better they would do better, that's just how it was.

From a very young age he had to grow "big boy shoulders" and was working from the beginning. Pig and calf runs, a milk run, selling papers, banana farming, you name it, my Dad had done it. Sadly he had to bury his own father when he was thirteen years old.

The times were harsh and they soldiered on, no matter what was thrown in their path.

He married at the age of 16 and had 5 kids well before he met my mum. The story is so interesting. We all have a story, and its good to get a background to see how it all fits in. When my parents came together, it was not without its issues. They had many things to deal with. The one thing about them, is that they stuck it out together through thick and thin and I honor them for that.

We must be grateful for the those that
that have walked before us, for each
generation paves way for the next.

Just before I turned 2, they adopted another baby, who was to be my sister, Roslyn. The day they brought her home from hospital, I don't know if I looked too happy at the time, there was a photo of me with a long look on my face.

"What, I am not going to be the center of attention any more? Darn!"

We were lucky to have such caring and loving parents to raise us, they really looked after us and loved us like their own flesh and blood.

Our parents gave us this poem, Mum typed it out and Dad got these little gold frames to put it in. I still have it to this day.

NOT FLESH OF OUR FLESH
NOR BONE OF OUR BONE
BUT STILL MIRACULOUSLY OUR OWN
NEVER DOUBT FOR EVER A MINUTE
YOU WERE NOT BORN UNDER OUR HEART
BUT IN IT...
Author (unknown)

Some of my earliest memories were of accompanying my dad and selling raffle tickets at the local rugby league football club, proudly perched high on top of his shoulders, and of eating cookies and cake at Nanna and Granddad's in Palm Beach with my sister Roslyn. We were always so bugged eyed when we knew there was treats to be had. No matter how much we ate at lunch, there was always room for Nanna's cookies. Our family travelled many a mile up and down the beaches in our four-wheel drive searching for fish. Dad was honorary beach warden at The Southport Spit and we would be at the ocean often. Love, laughs and plenty of travels, and of course, sport! What would I have done without sport? I started at a young age and thankfully blessed with some natural talent to play with. Both my sister and I were involved in Little Athletics and Netball, both representing the state at National Level.

(FAMILY SPAGHETTI OUTING....MANY MOONS AGO)

At ten years of age, my horizons expanded when we travelled around Australia in a Land Rover, Mum and Dad in the front, us 2 kids in the back. We met up with another family in Western Australia and continued with them for the rest of the trip. It was such a great time, having the opportunity to see Australia and be out of school and still learning!

The next significant travel throughout my early years was representing Queensland in Track and Field and Netball, I got to go to places like Darwin, Alice Springs, Adelaide, Melbourne, Perth and Sydney.

All through high school Dad drove both of us girls everywhere for our sport, right until driving age and then I was taking myself the hour drive up to Brisbane four times a week for Netball training and games. A significant trip for me was one Friday night in 1990. It was a turning point in my sport, but more significantly, the path I was about to embark on in my life.

CHAPTER 2

The Power of Change

I felt that there was divine intervention right there and then. It was the State Netball selection trials. I had made the teams the last couple of years, and this would have been my debut into Open competition for Nationals. Unfortunately at the time, I was not selected, even though I had played well and scored well. It was a real shock to the system. Everyone, including myself were surprised that my name was not announced to the team. Even some of the girls who made the team were in disbelief.

I was feeling angry and overcome with disappointment. I couldn't believe it and uncharacteristically expressed outward emotion by very loudly yelling what I thought of the sport. There was no hold back. I left the venue very upset. A deep chord within was struck, feelings of disbelief, failure, disappointment, and mostly rejection. It all came out, I bawled for the entire hour long drive back to the Gold Coast.

It was a huge shift for me and it brought out so much emotion. In hindsight, this experience was doing exactly what it was meant to. This was all in divine alignment.

My Mum and Dad were both in their usual place on the couch watching television when I entered the room, trying to hold back tears. They felt the pain of my disappointment and consoled me as much as a parent can in those instances.

The intense feelings of rejection and disappointment of not being chosen for this team were enough stimulus for me to switch sports, and just few weeks later outrigger canoeing had snuck its way into my life. My best friend Kylie invited me to join her to try outrigger paddling one Sunday morning with the Surfers Paradise Outrigger Canoe Club. This happening changed my whole world.

Paddling the canoe felt quite natural and I took to it like a duck to water. The movement and the fact I was on the water, made me feel very good very quickly. I decided to join the club, and after eight weeks of focused training, I was part of the winning crew at the Hamilton Island International Regatta held on the Great Barrier Reef.

Hundreds of paddlers from all over Australia, New Zealand, Hawaii, Tahiti and South East Asia come to Hamilton Island for four days of racing and partying at one of the major annual events of outrigger canoeing.

After winning our very first outrigger race here, my team made news headlines and had all sorts of media exposure. This was where it all started for me, and Hamilton Island became very much part of my life for the next 15 years.

The next thing I knew was that I am training full tilt for a World Championship Outrigger race in Hawaii later that year. It all happened so quickly, with much ease, but most of all with so much joy and absolutely no regrets.

CHAPTER 3

Aloha Hawaii

The warm air enveloped me as we disembark at the Honolulu International Airport. A feeling of being at home and a sense of calm came upon me. It felt very natural and comfortable for me. I was coming home. I have heard of many people experiencing this when they arrive in Hawaii for the first time.

Outrigger canoeing was a very natural transition for me. Physically, it was a familiar movement, even though I had not done it before. My body was made for it, and success in the sport happened rather quickly, which always keeps the momentum and motivation going. We placed fourth in our first Molokai Crossing, and my team Surfers Paradise were the first female crew from Australia to race at this event. It was only the second year in Australia that women had raced the Hamilton Cup, so I came into the sport very close to it's introduction Down Under.

Our group of girls were blazing the path for many more teams to come and experience this incredible race. I didn't know too much about it at the time, but paddling open ocean from one island to another is certainly an intriguing and challenging adventure.

The canoe is an equalizer, bringing people together, to a common place.

It doesn't work if you are out of sync, focused elsewhere or not pulling your weight. When everyone is dialed in body, mind and spirit, the canoe becomes the seventh paddler. We merge with the craft and become ONE.

Before the start of the Na Wahine O'Ke Kai, hundreds of women paddlers gather at Hale O Lono Harbor. As we all hold hands we are swiftly unified by a Hawaiian chant amplified over the loudspeaker. Goose bumps, chicken skin, that wave, comes over the body. Embraced by a feeling of spiritual peace and connection to something larger, a familiarity washes over me. That alone is enough to want to experience again, and again.

Our Surfers Paradise Outrigger crew took third place the next year. The year after I travelled to Europe and came through Newport Beach for a few weeks to train with the Offshore Canoe Club from California. We placed fourth. In 1993 our Surfers team placed third again, and then I didn't race the channel until three years later.

In the interim period I took up sprint kayaking and then in 1996 we competed as an Australian team, for Molokai, affectionately known as the "Riggeroos." I was fit and had a much stronger paddling base from the all the kayaking. Our Riggeroos team came second and the following year 1997, we became the first international crew to win the Women's Molokai World Championship, Na Wahine O'Ke Kai.

Our crew was a union of many talents and strengths. We all worked diligently, mostly on our own and then we would come together for practice each weekend. Some girls would fly up from Sydney. The rest of us were either based on the Gold Coast or the Sunshine Coast. The practices would alternate between these venues. The vision was set, the space was held and work was done. We had already won in my mind.

Then came the mystery and the unfolding. The letting go, the letting GOD.

We all secretly knew we could win. There were no words exchanged about this feeling. It was innate. It was cultivated through preparation and self belief. When we all came together, the energy was unstoppable. With that said, the universe threw some tests in there for us.

We had things stolen, luggage lost, all these little things were happening to distract us but we were not giving them full attention. We kept our focus.

As we paddled towards the finish line at the Hilton Hawaiian Village, there were hundreds of people lining the beach clapping, and the sound of drums and Hawaiian chanting greeted us as we crossed the line. Tears of joy and giggling inside, I couldn't believe it. We had won. Despite all those other things happening, this was the outcome. It was meant to be.

The Molokai race in 1998 was a different experience. We did not have the same confidence feeling going in. We didn't know this time. People knew who we were and the attention was on us. There was more energy to contend with. We were careful to not place too much pressure on ourselves.

The race was hard, so we had to work more this time to overcome external factors, mostly the mind. We didn't lead from the beginning. We just kept motoring on one stroke at a time. There was a point mid channel where we were racing another crew, who were level with us, but several hundred meters away to our right. I was sitting in two seat, the voice of canoe. Whilst calling the changes, the most incredible energy came over me and the rest the crew. We all felt it, and our strokes became stronger, the boat responded without words, we started to pull away from the other team. We were moving now. There was new motivation in every stroke. I am giggling as I write this and have the hugest grin on my face!

It was our dolphin friends! They came to assist. The pod was maybe 75-100 strong, the spinners! I so was overjoyed and happy to see them, to feel them. It was just what I needed in that moment. We all needed them. They were jumping and spinning right alongside our canoe, so close that I was worried I would hit one with my paddle.

When you are about three hours into a 6 hour race, it's very mental, you can drift in and out of focus as the body starts to feel the tiredness. You have conditioned the body but there is still the ebb and flow of energy as well as the changing current and conditions in the water.

The dolphins were right on cue. It was the highlight for me. We crossed the finish line first for the second year in a row. A sweet victory. That divine dolphin moment is etched in my memory. I so love those playful creatures!

The intention is balance...
Maintain the place where you are still in the joy so
the mind is kept at bay. Paddle for the love of it, stay
connected with your fellow traveller's and enjoy the ride.

CHAPTER 4

Recognition...

A fter the celebrations of that race and a little recovery time, a few of us took a trip to Kona to watch the Ironman Triathlon. It is here on the Big Island "something" is reignited in me.

One afternoon we take time to check out the stalls in the King Kamehameha Hotel. Many vendors are setting up and displaying their wares, the latest gadgets, superfoods and sports drinks. Along with the sports gear, there was a lovely Hawaiian woman threading leis.

I stopped to smell one of my favorite fragrances, the tuberose.

The woman was very friendly and greeted me with "Aloha" and continued to look at me quite closely, kind of like that feeling when you know someone but don't know their name. She asked me whether I was a canoe paddler and of course I answered yes. In the next breath she spoke these words.

"You relative, you relative." She was adamant, forehead all crunched and even pinching my cheeks with certainty. "Yes, you relative." She mentioned a particular Ohana several times. I quickly replied. "I don't think so, not me" shaking my head. "I am from Australia."

This is exactly where the proverbial penny dropped. My own words echoed back at me and then a wave of nervousness and fear engulfed me in that moment.

With an elder of Hawaiian culture, there is an unspoken respect. I knew deep inside that she was on the right track and not just talking story. I felt it.

My reaction was physical, the body knew, the pit of my stomach dropped and I walked outside rather quickly with my friends in tow. My memory was triggered back to the day my parents told me I was adopted, and the only information they had was that the mother was English and the father was Hawaiian. It is amazing how selective our memory is. That piece of information shared with me at an early age just took on a brand new significance.

I was overcome by fear, fear of the unknown, and then my identity was up for questioning.

"I am Aussie." I told the woman. I remember saying it with such conviction. A wall of protection came up immediately. I was trying desperately to hold on to who I knew myself to be, yet something had been awakened.

The afternoon was very "spacey" for me. I was laying low. I was so very happy my teammates, Sue and Cassandra were with me at the time. We talked a little about the interaction with the woman but I was really wanting to run and hide. I was being called out. Things about me started to make more sense, my love for Hawaii, the sense of belonging, the synchronicity that was occurring around me. Does this happen to everyone in Hawaii? It is a such a magical place, and it was a little overwhelming in a good way.

After recovering from the shock, I got on with the weekend. I slept a lot. There was enough distraction with the ironman race going that I didn't think about it again. It did however occupy space in the mind, and on return to Australia, I found myself becoming very curious. I fell in love with Hawaii the day I stepped foot on her. It was home to my whole being and I knew it.

CHAPTER 5

I feel different

After that trip, I threw myself back into kayak training. I was in great physical shape and spent much of my time paddling the canals of Mermaid Waters. My kayaking was the one thing that remained constant. My boat was like a home away from home, and life went on as normal. The racing and discipline of training for an Olympic sport ended up being the place for my personal growth. I learnt much about myself.

My partner at the time and I owned a house on the water, so it was easy to launch from the backyard. I loved paddling. It was a place to escape the endless thoughts of the mind, become clear, and have a great workout. Also through the sport, I met many people and made friends from around the globe. The Swedish Team would come for training camp, and I would spend time with them, so easy, so natural. I definitely had an affinity with the European cultures. We had a lovely paddler come stay with us from Denmark. He was on the Danish National team.

It was a wonderful thing to have a common interest and immediately feel the sense of family. I must say, something tweaked my soul with this connection. It was very familiar. Wasn't real sure of what it was but it kind of felt like he was someone from my past or even a messenger of my future.

I feel that there certain souls that are placed on our path with the clues, kind of a realignment point. I am certain of this.

He was the second person to cross my path and spark my being on a deep level. Something triggered for me. It felt cultural and deep. We would drink tea and talk.

He was a true gift on this path and I feel subconsciously this Danish connection I had made was no coincidence. There was definitely a higher reason. Maybe our ancestors were talking story. The European part of me was awakened.

*I wonder with our lives, and the unfolding,
do we drop a breadcrumb trail just so we
can adventure and find our way back
home? Are we living our life backwards?*

*If we are a soul in embodiment, there is an all
knowing aspect to our self that exists somewhere
within us. Once we take a body and descend
to this earthly plane, we are born again, most
often with divine forgetfulness, so we can
journey, learn the lessons we came to learn and
ultimately remember who we are at our essence.*

*When we feel the connection with certain
people on our path, it is our soul, knowing and
bringing the connection to our awareness.*

CHAPTER 6

Europe Calls

I was working with my partner in a boat building company, helping him in the office, making paddles, and getting the kayaks ready for distribution locally, interstate and abroad. He worked very hard and I assisted where possible. The factory where we were each day, was a hub of activity and a common meeting place for the paddlers.

People would drop by during the day to check out equipment or just pop in for a chat. It was a paddling lifestyle. I often felt I had put myself in his shadow and was content to take a backseat role. He was the Olympic medallist in our abode, and I was striving in that direction, the best way I could. There was a part of me that was playing the proving myself program, and eventually it wore me down. I was trying so hard, and went through countless mind trips of not feeling good enough because I wasn't paddling fast enough like the others.

Athletes must be extremely careful of not placing their self worth as a human being on their performance alone. It is very unbalanced. Being in that field was definitely the ideal place for learning and have self worth issues come up.

I knew that wasn't who I was, that's why I kept going. I really just loved to paddle. The competition and the training game was quite intense for me to tell the truth.

It was interesting how I found myself with this group of very determined, competitive high achievers, all successful in their own right. The ultimate goal in sport as I knew it to be was to compete at Olympic level, and everyone I paddled with was aiming for this, and some had even won medals in the past. There was for sure the impetus and motivation with this group to achieve success, and no doubt that mindset has helped me further down the track in my personal endeavors.

Kayaking did not come naturally to me and I spent a long time perfecting technique and desiring to paddle faster. My strength was always in a team boat with others, and I was fortunate enough to win a National K4 title which was the most memorable experience of my racing career.

We were at the Olympic Regatta Course in Penrith Lakes, Sydney and one of the girls in the four was injured. I was without a crew and received a last minute call up to race. We had one practice the afternoon before, and the next morning our crew tied for first place in the final against the four fastest girls on paper in the country. That year in the K1 I was ninth overall in the country. It was the best I had done. The girls were really fast. I enjoyed boxing with a top trainer twice weekly, and physically was the fittest I had ever been. I trained amongst some of the best paddlers in the world, so it was a pressure cooker for me in a sense.

I enjoyed the discipline of training. I loved the level of physical prowess I was experiencing and that was the joy for me. I was finally moving into a better place with it all, not so much comparing and judging myself with others. It is a little hard when you are in the competitive environment! I strived to be my best, but finally without the attachment of having to "make it" to the top. If I was to make it, then that would be a bonus.

If I was to be close to making my first national team for kayaking it would have been this particular year. I was enjoying my progress and was inspired to keep training through the off season. There was an opportunity to train and race in Sweden for the summer, so I decided to go. It was to be eight weeks in total and was the first time I had gone to do something just for me. I wasn't attached to a team I was solo and exploring more of myself in that competitive arena.

There was no expectation, no pressure on myself. I went for the pure joy of racing and training. I really just wanted to see how fast I could go, no proving to anyone, just for the fun of it. I was away from family, from partner and finding my way as best as I could. My confidence in myself grew. It was about finding my own identity. Being somewhere completely different, where no one knew who I was, or my story, and I could create freely and be who I wanted to be within this experience.

CHAPTER 7

Waking up

The following year, 1999 I was experiencing random bursts of emotion.

I didn't understand what was happening and my partner truly had no idea. I found it difficult to communicate and would often feel weird and lost at times. I was seeking knowledge and awareness from a Human Potentials Group. This was a great help initially and provided tremendous support during this time. It was a safe place for me to process and my spiritual awareness was opening. Things were shifting.

I was yearning for a sense of connection at the core of my being and there were parts of me rising to the surface that had depth and mystery to them. I longed to get back to Hawaii, and an opportunity came to paddle the Molokai Channel with Offshore, California.

This team had won the channel ten times. They boasted one of the best steerers in the world. I was honored to be asked and I jumped at the opportunity. I had raced with them seven years before so I knew the core of the paddlers on the team. I met them on Oahu, we had a few paddles together, then we were back out paddling on the Ka'iwi Channel doing what we loved. After this trip I did not visit the islands for three years and much happened in the interim.

In those three years away from Hawaii, I would have regular Lomi Lomi massage treatments which were beneficial to my physical training but also relaxed me enough to feel and be in tune with my greater source. These treatments were powerful. Massage, bodywork and the Lomi became a major focus for me and so then the peeling of the layers began, like an onion they say.

The body has its own program and the emotions that we experience can get locked in the body. I guess I was being peeled open and unlocked!

I liked being an athlete as it gave me the excuse to have regular massage, not that we need an excuse. It helped the mind to justify it. I was regularly looked after by Big Al who has a happy family of many people who have been seeing him for years. That is where I learnt the most. By receiving regularly, the body learns from the movements and there is certainly a transmission of some sort taking place. During these times I visited a Chiropractor who was also a Kinesiologist. This really changed the course of my life. I was experiencing so much emotion, crying at night for no reason, I was not able to discern the mindset I was in and things were switching on in my body. I was getting enough nudges to do something about it and take some action. I believe now this was part of an awakening process.

My athletic career turned into my healing journey. Obviously something was overriding the competitive drive. God was prioritizing.

Most people are conscious of this and aware, others are still waking up to the correlation between health and spirit. I know that spirit won this race with me, and it was my health indicators that started to reveal this part of my life:

Athlete + pushing body hard + pressure to
perform + always looking for more
= eventual overload and things boiling up and
seeking attention, acknowledgment

CHAPTER 8

Relief

I remember walking into Doctor Keith's Chiropractic clinic some years prior and he asked me so simply. "What is troubling you, Robyn?" Oh boy, I just started to cry, and couldn't stop, he just sat there quietly with a caring and compassionate look on his face until I stopped. He didn't try console me. He just let me be and allowed the process.

A few minutes later I could breathe again. I felt much lighter. Just to have a safe space to let go provided so much relief to me. The body needed to release the energy. I would receive regular adjustments from then on. There was so much shifting in my awareness, and in any case, my health was important to me and I did what I needed to at the time. The body was my compass and was guiding the way.

After all the bodywork and massage, it was only fitting that I learn some more so I went to Massage School. I was also attuned for Reiki I and II (form of energy healing) then naturally I began working on people. Health and wellness and anything to do with it became a focus, I was immersed in books, articles and enjoyed learning about our body. I witnessed such contrast around me. With my parents not well, it set off stimulus to learn and take care of the body.

I knew it was my responsibility, my vehicle to maintain so to speak.

With the motivation of improving and being the best I could be, I was always interested to explore the deeper or metaphysical cause. It fascinated me, and when the emotional stuff would clear, the physical body would free up some more. I became very in tune with myself and realized the interconnection of the many levels of our being.

If you are a human being you are on some sort of healing journey whether you know it or not, some of us are active and consciously doing it, others are not even aware and do not pursue further. All is as it is. If you hear the call, you go, you do...

Our responsibility is to understand, accept
and love who we are, all parts of us.
Self love is the ticket home.

CHAPTER 9

The Race of Life

Within those three years away from Hawaii, my Dad suffered a heart attack.

He didn't even know it happened. We got him to the hospital in time thankfully, and then it was diagnosed. Double by pass heart surgery was scheduled immediately.

On the same day that Dad was scheduled for surgery, My sister and I were both on the Surfers Paradise crew to paddle in the Gold Coast Cup a 40 km Outrigger race from Coolangatta to the Southport Spit.

We were not in the mood to race. The girls were going to have to find two other paddlers.

The day before the surgery, Mum was encouraging us to race. She said knowingly to us, "Your father would want you to race." She was right. Was more people worrying the best thing or was it better for us girls to be out on the ocean doing something we love but this time with a far greater intention? It would be healthy to have the support of our teammates around us for sure.

It was very hard to come to this decision, but we as a family, decided that Rozi and I should do the race that morning for Dad, in his honor. We could only pray he would pull through and be okay.

The girls were happy with our decision and understood the significance of the race for us. They supported us and became an important energetic link for us and for Dad. We were putting on our brave faces preparing for the race of life. At the hospital our father was being prepared for open heart surgery.

There were plenty of nerves that morning but not for the race. The canoe race was nothing, in comparison to what was happening in our life. However, the event proved to be just the medicine needed for everyone. It was all connected.

We were all connected. Both my sister and I were quite numb with the experience. It was just our bodies going through the motions, our heart and mind were elsewhere. The girls were carrying us in one way, but in another way, we were providing them with a bigger goal, a bigger intention, a bigger motivation for racing that day.

Our team was tight, keeping focused together and very much to ourselves. Every stroke was important, every breath was important and the positive energy we were creating amongst us was radiating where it needed to I am sure of this.

My sister and I would well up with tears periodically during the race, especially if we happened to look at one another. Very quickly we would be pulled back to task and to the present moment of paddling, focusing on one stroke at a time.

I can't even remember the race. Three hours went by so fast. Our crew paddled around the seaway wall in first position, we were powering so hard, giving it our all and ended up winning the race. Back on shore, the whole team was in tears. We did it. We now were hoping Dad pulled through on his side. We spoke to mum on the phone immediately after the race and the surgery was successful, Dad was going to be okay, and we couldn't wait to see him.

The canoe brings to us so many gifts.
A vehicle for healing, for learning.
A safe vessel for the journey at hand.

CHAPTER 10

I quit

O ne particular morning we were doing six minute pieces on the canal in Mermaid Waters and I was doing well riding the wash of Katrin and Anna our European imports. Then it became such a struggle, I was hanging on for dear life and it was not joyful. Theres a difference. When the body is conditioning itself and you are in alignment in mind and spirit, then all is well. I was so out of alignment forcing it all.

These girls were Olympic medallist twice fold and raised the standard of paddling here in Australia when they arrived some years before. Now here I was, with all my other things brewing, still trying to play the game, still TRYING to keep up. My spirit was calling the shots. I literally ran out of gas that morning. The inner voice was saying, "No. That's enough. Stop right there. You don't have to do this anymore. It's done, give it up. Don't do it like this."

I remember stopping my paddle and letting my boat glide to a complete halt before the six minute piece was finished. I was sitting in my boat bobbing up and down on the waves with my paddle slumping over the cockpit in numbness. I wondered what all this was for. The pushing, the struggle? I was so over it and not happy. My time here was up. It was indeed. My lovely German coach came over in the motor boat and asked me what happened. "I quit I have had enough" I said. He was so neutral and replied with a compassionate tone. "That is okay, YOU are fine."

I felt much freedom morning. The truth was spoken. My being was not enjoying what I was putting myself through. After voicing and taking action in that moment, I had a new sense of excitement come over me. I came alive. Spirit was happy. The reset button on my computer had been pressed.

CHAPTER 11

Reset

Three days later, after not going near my boat or on the water, I went back to practice. I felt so different and had the sense of "I AM" in charge. Not me, the personality or ego. I felt like my spirit was now calling the shots. I was paddling with a whole new attitude and I no longer felt the pressure on myself that I paddled with for so long. I had to quit from the place of the mind and reconnect to the whole activity through my heart. I was totally caught up in a game that wasn't even me. By quitting, I declared a reset for myself. Now I was able to paddle with a new sense of freedom and really be true to myself without the pressure of comparison and judgment. This time I just did my own thing. If it was to be my path, it would unfold.

When I first started kayaking I was in my mid twenties and I was paddling with fourteen year olds who were absolutely kicking my butt in practices. My initial experience and introduction to the sport was rather humbling. This sport woke me up. It woke my spirit up through experiences that were not in alignment with my being. I also learnt that I could do it my way, and really enjoy the process and whether I went to the Olympics or not didn't come into the equation.

I could now paddle for me and my own enjoyment and self improvement, not for anyone else and certainly not use paddling as a vehicle to prove my worth.

"We all have our own Olympics to participate in.
Experiences come our way as an opportunity
to overcome and to remember our true nature,
our true essence, our larger SELF."
It's part of remembrance.

CHAPTER 12

Truth

My partner and I decided to go our separate ways, I had changed. We had to honor our truths.

The love was always there. It doesn't go away. The expression of it shifts and moves, and if you are not on the same page as your partner then its very difficult to continue in the same way. We shared many moments of life together, and I feel so blessed for that. I have grown because of him. He is part of me. No one is separate. We merge with one another and become all the more whole because of this. He was honest and would always speak his truth, no matter how harsh it may have been to the other party.

You knew where you stood with him. He was very much like my Dad, no surprises there.

One morning, we woke up together and pondered the question "Was our time up?"

Looking at one another and nodding with deep acknowledgement, it was.

We were not really sure of what to do next. Our circle of friends were surprised and shocked, however, we didn't fight it, some may have judged us for not trying harder, giving it another chance. We did try, however it was not it. We were in the "Try" phase and attempting for the new but had no way of navigating this place at the time. On a larger scale, for us to evolve and to grow parting ways was the answer at the time.

I know in my heart it was a huge decision, and I just trusted. It gave me feelings of pain, and grief, it brought doubt, but I kept moving forward, with nothing but a tiny shred of innate wisdom, knowing deep down that I was doing the right thing.

CHAPTER 13

Ikaika

One of the girls I paddled and raced against at the kayak regattas was very different to most of the competitors. Shelley was very positive and friendly. She was not in it for the reason other than purely loving what she did and taking joy from the activity, I liked this, and even though she was one of the top girls, she was also happened to be one of the friendliest on the water.

Shelley paddled outriggers in Sydney and was part of the winning crew for Molokai in 1998 with me. She also knew of my adoption and was always fascinated and interested in any updates I had for her. Both she and her husband Guy were very supportive of me and inspired me greatly on my journey.

In 2002 she put together a crew to race Molokai which consisted of a few girls from Queensland and a few from New South Wales. The team was called "Ikaika" in Hawaiian this translates as "Strength." We trained as two separate groups interstate, sometimes we would be only four in a boat and we were always so happy when the girls from the local club would come to fill in for us and make up the extra seats.

After many cold winter workouts it was time to travel to Hawaii. I was bubbling with excitement, it had been a while. Our flight from Australia arrived into Honolulu late at night.

The next morning we walked from the hotel in Waikiki directly to the ocean. It was ritual. Before we did any training or anything, it was time to have that moment, submerging the body, being embraced by the warm water, washing off our worries and all it took to get here again. Honoring this beautiful land. The morning ocean blessing is highly recommended on your arrival here.

After breakfast we paddled out from the Anuenue club in Waikiki. It is located by the lagoon at the Hilton Hawaiian Village which is where the race finishes. Our other training sessions were held from the Outrigger Canoe Club, and the most fun was when we got to do a practice change session from the Hui Nalu Canoe Club in Hawaii Kai. Our new friends Tim and Maggie provided a motor boat, and Maggie drove it for us this day.

I had met this couple through the paddling circles some years before. Maggie is so full of life, always ready for activity. Whether it be surfing, hiking, paddling, she is full of beans and would run up Koko Head which for those that don't know is a stair climb that goes straight up for just under a mile. It's not a walk in the park that's for sure. Maggie could do that twice in a row! Her husband Tim, who is a very accomplished paddler and waterman, was never far from her side and they would often paddle races together, a very good team.

It was lovely of them to help us out. We had a wonderful morning paddling down past Portlock, along the rock wall. The clear deep blue water was inviting, and we had no trouble jumping in off the boat for the changes. The temperature so warm in comparison to what we were experiencing back in Australia. We were happy about that.

The girls who had not been to Hawaii before were beside themselves. It is always so much fun to have newbies on the team. Their fresh energy infused the experienced group and we saw it all through new eyes again. A whole new experience and the channel became a different race each time. After training that day, we made our usual preparations for the race, getting water and race supplies. The next morning we would be taking a one way flight to Molokai.

Race day arrived and it was another awesome day on the water. Deep blue seas, moderate wind and swell, and plenty of malolo (flying fish)

We all love the water so much, it's hard not to be smiling. We paddled our best and ended up in fifth place.

Once the race was done, we were looking forward to some play time. Our new friends Mike and Jimmy, entertained us for the next few days with canoe surfing, a little dancing and lot of laughter along the way. We piled into the back of Jimmy's truck and he ferried us about the town. It was a fun time. We were so grateful for the wonderful hospitality of our friends.

Just before this short trip was to end, we had a last minute invite to a birthday party. It was for our new friend Tim. It was fancy dress and our spontaneity left us a little underdone in the costume department. The party was held at a beautiful oceanfront property just walking distance from the Outrigger Club.

Ocean glistening in the background, fabulous music, great food and new friends, it boasted all the ingredients for a fabulous party. The birthday boy was extremely happy to have his large family all together and to celebrate with his friends. There were many people, and I knew quite a few from paddling. Our friends Mike and Stu played wonderful Hawaiian music, and we sang and danced through the night.

Little did I know at the time but this party was to be a significant turning point, a giant piece in the puzzle of my life to date.

There are no coincidences and spirit
works in the funniest of ways...
"We are always being guided."

CHAPTER 14

Sharing Intention

O n my return to Australia, I went back to school to teach
year nine Physical Education and year eight Computer
Studies. I ended up there by way of a position opening up that
was tailor made for my experience and qualifications. My friend
was a paddler and a teacher, and she was leaving and needed to
fill the position. It was a Sports Excellence school so I taught in
the Kayak Program. I didn't know much about computers to tell
the truth, but we learn through teaching something right? That
was my hope.

The Kayaking Sports Excellence Program was a great initia-
tive. It was one of a kind. The school was very instrumental with
sport and creative arts and students had an opportunity to really
excel in their chosen areas. My mentor coach and teacher in the
program was inspirational. He had a huge heart and passion for
the sport and started so many people on the water by sharing the
gift of paddling. I worked with John for four years and then took
the program over when he left. It was a wonderful opportunity
and experience for me and I met some very talented and gifted
teachers.

I was fortunate to be out on the water regularly with the kids
and loved interacting with these bright beings! We had some
great mornings on Currumbin Estuary where on occasion dolphins would be present and playing amongst our kayaks. When

it was very calm we would paddle the K1's outside the alley and float out in the open ocean, a beautiful and truly a blessed experience for us all. If that was a regular Monday morning at school, then I was more than happy to be on duty.

I usually spent some of the weekends with my parents, and even though Dad was not well, we would on occasion take the hour long drive to Potsville or Byron Bay for lunch.

One particular Sunday we decided to stay local and went to a little place called Cafe Magic. It figures...

It was time to start my search for my birthparents and I was needing to share.

I was ready to go into action and with my Mum and Dad's blessing would go ahead with the process. It seemed right and natural to tell them. I shared over lunch my intention. They expressed their support and told me that they expected this would happen at some point in my life. The big question then was whether I would be okay with doing this. I wonder about the birthparents. What effect would it have on them? After all, it has been thirty-six years.

Telling my parents was important to me. I was glad to get it off my chest. I had the habit of making sure it was okay with everyone. I have since learned that I have to make sure its okay with me before I do anything. I used to be the pleaser of all! We learn.

I had set a goal to know my biological roots, and finally after the last trip to Hawaii, "something" had prompted me to take action.

Before the year was out, I wrote to the State Adoption Department. The paper trail is not the most fun process but nevertheless, a process. It was time. Nothing else I was doing was fulfilling this curiosity. Spirit was calling the shots and I was listening.

CHAPTER 15

Receiving Notice
"Who am I?"

I t was a typical routine day, with the alarm going off at 5.30am, just a short drive to practice, and on the water by 6am. This particular morning after our session, I was meeting one of my training partners for breakfast in Nobby Beach. It was a favorite place for all the paddlers after training, because they knew us well and knew our orders. Before breakfast I went to check my mail box which was just near the cafe. I crouched down, put the key in and opened to find a wad of envelopes, quickly flicking through I noticed one from the Queensland Government.

I knew what it was, and my stomach was overtaken with nervous energy. I didn't want to open it there on my own, I was afraid of what it may say, good or bad, I just did not want to experience this by myself. My paddler friend Andrea pulled into the parking space in front of the post office where I was standing. She came towards me, and I shakily showed her the envelope and told her what it was. I planned to open it once we got to the table. This was such a strange sensation. One way or another there was some news in that envelope.

Formally typewritten it was a response to my requesting information regarding my biological parents. It was a copy of a birth extract. It had my full name and the name of my birthmother. I was born "Louisa" and my birthmothers name was Astrid.

My cells were bubbling as I was reading. It seemed that anything that I ever knew about who I was, happened to be double taking inside of me. "Oh my god, I was called someone completely different." A myriad of feelings were running through me. It was a quiet revelation inside.

Having my friend with me was a blessing. This was not something I was about to shout to the world at this point. Why? It just didn't feel right to do so.

Not yet anyway. I felt quite strange at this time. It said that the mother was born in Surabaya, Indonesia? I was incredibly curious as I contemplated my next move. I took my time in allowing things to register and integrate.

I can't recall whether I told my parents straight away, I think not. I was mindful of their feelings and aware of the various issues it can bring forth.

There are multitude of perspectives in the area of adoption, issues with the biological parent's, the adopted child and the adoptive parents, holy cow, that's quite a bundle there. From an energetic perspective, I was tired just thinking about it. The adoption people had a whole pamphlet on it! I questioned whether I was up for all that. I guess I was.

Once you set an intention and go into inspired action, the universe provides a domino effect.

From the cafe with the letter in hand I drove home. Just knowing that information changed my perspective, yet the curiosity remained. Who was this woman that gave birth to me? Surabaya, Indonesia? That's where she was born was interesting in itself. I wondered what it all meant?

Back at my parent's house, I showed them the letter. It was very strange giving it to them. Their reaction was not surprising, fairly matter of fact. Mum was fine. However my Dad was a little apprehensive. She later expressed to me that he was feeling that way. My father was very sensitive like myself and I knew how he was feeling. I found myself playing the news down somewhat. As human beings, we have a tendency to do this, it's a protective mechanism. Unfortunately, it just holds it all in place. We think we know how someone will feel, but we can also be caught in projecting our own thoughts, or perceptions upon another.

After I told them, I went to the park next door to their house. There were swings. I was happy to swing, something I love to do when the opportunity arises.

A gentle breeze in my face, the kookaburras laughing in the background, I was enjoying the sensation of freedom and allowing the mornings events to sink in.

I didn't act on that information immediately. There were other things going on. It is a little freaky to think you were someone else. The mind was having some reservations. The questions were surfacing. What now? What do I do with this information?

That paper found its way to into a folder and it got filed with my other adoption papers for the time being. I wondered who the father was. Was he really from Hawaii like my parents had been told? The only way to find out was to contact the birthmother.

It was many months before I did anything else. The emotions needed processing and timing is a factor. The universe has a way of lining things up once an idea or desire is set in motion and all the puzzle pieces have a chance to be put in place. This is not our job to do. I was in the "pause" breath, the one we talk about in yoga, where you are in the pose, you're breathing, then when you finally come out of the pose, there's the moment of a pause, time to reflect and feel.

In my experience I have known that when you ask for something, miracles can start happening. One pebble thrown in a lake sends ripples and reverberates out to reach many shores.

I had thrown the pebble and the rippling was definitely in motion.

After receiving my birthmother's name, it was about four months later until I explored further. I was not ready for the next step in meeting her at that point. We don't get given the "why" straight away. It's a feeling or an innate knowing. When "something" doesn't feel quite right, we must honor that.

In hindsight, she had a lot going on in that time. We do sense these things, so rather than anguish over indecisiveness and wait, I was going to have some fun. That was the intention. I often wondered where my birth father was and on which island. Obviously I had nothing to go on until I found out from the mother, but for a divine reason it was not time.

CHAPTER 16

The European in me

There was much European influence around me with our German friends and in particular Katrin, who came to Australia to paddle for the green and gold. She was someone I really enjoyed conversing with. We would talk on over coffee and cake in her beachside apartment. I really enjoyed this connection and our talks were of a worldly and global nature. She was the best paddler in Australia and an Olympic silver and bronze medallist for both countries. She was a professional athlete, and I so liked her lifestyle, I tried it for a while.

In about March of 2003 Katrin was leaving for Europe for a summer of competition and training. She asked if I would like to stay at her place by the beach. I was certainly ready for a little more feminine energy, the ocean and my own space, it was time for Robyn.

It's so interesting to look back at the journey and the people and places, none of which felt like home to me. It was just somewhere on the way. I definitely was not at home in myself, which was not surprising given the circumstances.

The beachside unit was very clean and orderly. It was a nurturing place for my spirit and I could hear and see the ocean. Every day I would visit the beach even if it was just to go and say hello. Her unit was located on the esplanade in Mermaid Beach, not far from where I had first lived. She had a lovely chaise lounge with a reading lamp, positioned right near the window. I spent much time there reading and contemplating.

One of the fun things I loved doing while staying there was to use her bread maker. I would set the thing up the night before, put the mix in, set the timer to be done by 6.30am and by 7 when I had come home from paddling, the smell of the fresh bread would waft through the unit. I absolutely loved coming home to this smell.

It was incredibly nurturing for me to be there. Having the freedom and room for myself made such a huge difference to my being. There was the chance to get in touch with my needs at the time. I was there for a good 3 months before my next adventure.

CHAPTER 17

Budding Joy

Maintaining the annual racing routine, I ended up going to Hamilton Island for the regatta in June. When I returned there was another week at school before a two week winter break. I was restless after the Hamilton trip. I was so happy to see my friends. They were dropping hint to come to Hawaii for a holiday. Normally I would brush it off, but something was pulling me to just go. I checked the tickets, price was good, I was off school and it felt right. All I needed to do was move my things out of the unit so Katrin could return while I was in Hawaii. The few things I had went into storage at my parents house.

I emailed my friend Paula and told her I was visiting Honolulu. Paula and Chris have always opened their home to me, and have been very instrumental in my journey. I regard them as my 'hanai' or extended family.

The downstairs room has housed many of us girls over the years, we are like the extra daughters that they don't have.

My friend Sarah was also gracious in having me stay with her on Maui. It was a holiday but it was also such a natural transition to just turn up and fall into the groove of life. It would not be uncommon to get picked up from the airport, put a suit on and go for a paddle. There was no thinking, just a "get out and go." I like that.

Arriving this time was no different. It was my birthday how-ever, and after already celebrating in Australia and having a day stop in Fiji, when I got to Honolulu it was time to celebrate again. It was still the 2nd of July.

Chris and Paula took me to dinner at the Outrigger Canoe Club, which became a home base for me and I met many new friends by visiting and paddling from the club. It was an honor to be welcomed there. I felt very much at home, especially because paddling is held in such high regard. My life was paddling, and it was certainly a natural fit for me to be there.

Part of my fitness regime whilst there was paddling surf ski a few mornings a week with a group, and then every Monday night were time trials for the men's practice. It was about 8-10mile and a regular event. I felt very much at ease. Being out on the ocean with so many talented paddlers was very motivating and it also allowed me to feel rather safe so I could work on my paddle skills. It was also fun to be there for Outrigger's fourth of July cel-ebrations and attend their regatta. The morning of the regatta all the paddlers gathered as one big team and Walter, who is a friend and long time respected paddler and member of the club, gave a great pep talk and got everyone fired up for the races. I walked down with the team to Waikiki feeling very much part of the action!

When the races finished, many a water craft gathered about a mile offshore. The unofficial event is affectionately known as "The Flotilla." People were on blow up toys, surf mats, boards, canoes, really anything that floated. I was smiling so much that day, being out on the water looking at Diamond Head and think-ing, "Wow, I am so lucky to be here. This is so much fun."

My friend Malia and I were on a paddle board together mov-ing between the various groups of people partying out there. After a couple of hours at the flotilla, it was time to make our way back to the Outrigger. I hastily grabbed on to a sailing canoe that was going in that direction and we started moving very fast. Malia was holding on to me and the board and we made it all the way back to the club. It was probably a couple of miles.

There was no way I was letting go. We laughed so hard and as the speed increased, the water sprayed in our faces the whole way back. I am very lucky my biceps held up.

The memories that I have are very much of fun and joy. But behind that, I was in a time of transition and change. I felt very much at home in Hawaii, having fun, unaware of what was unfolding.

CHAPTER 18

Maui

There was an opportunity to visit Maui and stay with Sarah, so I decided that would be a fun thing to do. She picked me up from the airport and very soon after that, we were on canoes in the waters off Kihei. What a beautiful scene with the majestic Haleakala in the background overseeing us all, I always feel that the dormant volcano mountain is a "she" and I nickname her "Mother Maui." I found this island to be extremely nurturing to my soul. Everywhere we turned there was more beauty, and the clarity and color of the water was exquisite.

My friend is such a playful soul we had a lot a fun and I was happy to be there taking in the island delights. She lived near the beach and not far from the Wailea Canoe Club. I was lucky to be able to practice with her team and race a regatta. Little did I know I would be spending my summer doing more of that very thing.

Sarah owned property on Maui and had a couple retail stores, she was a real "goer" as we say in Australia, I was in awe of all she was doing, it was a lot, so it felt good to be able to assist her in small ways, to make her days a little easier. I found joy in that at the time. She would work during the day, I would take the car and sightsee, shop or whatever, and then at night, we would share a meal and talk story as you do!

It was getting toward the end of my time on Maui and then nearly time to return to Oz but I was getting such strong guidance and feeling to stay longer. Wondering how I was going to follow that guidance was eating me up a little, and some tension was building. I had teaching to go back to, back to life in that place where there is limbo, because we don't know what's next or the timing is not right. Everything in my being was telling me to stay. How could this work? I had no idea. What would I do if I stayed? What would my parents say? What would school say? How could I leave just like that without notice of intention?

Oh my, the monkey mind was going off! All these questions, yet within all of that was this incredible calm and knowing presence. I decided to tap into that feeling some more.

Night times on Maui, I experience an incredible "stillness." "Mother Maui," Haleakala was close by. This feeling was so steady and solid for me. It wasn't coming from any other person. It's like I was tuning in to the land that I was upon, and it was just doing its thing, being still, solid, present and all knowing. As I write this I recognize this part of me that is most prevalent when I am in nature. Through all this, nature has been my guiding light.

No one out there can give you the answers.
They can suggest, they can guide
but ultimately you are it,
and what I have learned is that we do know.
It's recognizing and allowing this knowing to be,
and the more you acknowledge it,
the more it can come forth.

Of course I am human and naturally at this point was needing some advice, so I called my dear friend Mike. He is a very bright being, intelligent, lighthearted, and is a pilot, so I know him to have quite good logic and judgement. He and I have had many a deep conversation on various topics, and there is a real ease and natural way about how we relate. I am sure we have had time together in other lives, as with many of these people in my story, but that would be another book!

I phoned Mike on Oahu to ask his opinion. He encouraged me to stay and go about things in a methodical manner. Mike asked all the right questions to see where I was. He was a great sounding board. He suggested that I stay the whole summer and paddle, do Molokai and then go home after that. I liked that suggestion and could envision that happening.

The next step was to contact my supervising teacher. I rang John on the Gold Coast and told him how I was feeling. He suggested I apply for emergency leave for the whole term. That would be the easiest way and it would be officially called 'stress' leave. I think if I didn't take leave then yes, it would be stress!

I had to overcome the "feeling guilty program" for doing something that I was needing. I felt like I was leaving everyone in the lurch, but it really wasn't like that all. I chose to look at it differently. This can be win-win for everyone. Somebody had just been given a whole term of work teaching and coaching my kayak kids out on the water. It was a great opportunity. They would be happy with this. Once I started getting my head around it all, it was time to call my parents and let them know my plans.

Just before making the call home, I had decided that I would take leave from school and just make it happen. I knew, with every ounce of my being, I was to stay in Hawaii longer. It just did not feel right to go back to Australia so soon.

I also knew, with this phone call my 'knowingness' would be put to the test.

I rang from Maui and spoke to Mum first, telling her all the things I had been up to, and she was always so happy to hear of my adventures and knew if I was happy or not. I shared my thoughts and my decision to stay longer and without any protest, she just rounded up the conversation and said, "I will put your father on the phone"

So here I am a grown women with this underlying fear of whether what I am proposing to do will be accepted. The permission program. When I look back, it was like talking to another aspect of myself, giving myself permission to do what my heart was yearning to do, got to love it huh. Human stuff.

I told Dad that I was going to stay until the end of the term. I was met with apprehension and disappointment. It was a little bit of a shock, but I allowed him to express and listened as best as I could beyond the words. As tough as my Dad appeared, he had an extremely soft and sensitive side and I could tell he was not entirely happy about my choice. I don't like to project, however, he may have been worried about losing me to Hawaii prematurely, and knowing that my biological father is somewhere in the islands, that, I am certain was at the back of his mind.

Fear was creeping in.

I don't know how we got through that phone call but we did. He for some reason was taking it very personally. He thought I was leaving him. When I started the search, curiosity was the initial spark, and now I felt like I was a traitor. Strange but that's how it felt. This is not wrong. The whole experience triggered the feeling of guilt. Best clear that one, I thought.

I have no blame for this, and so grateful that years prior I started my own self healing, which allowed me to clear much of those base emotional charges so they were not triggered as strongly, yet I could see what was going on. It was up to me to stay in that place of love, regardless of what was being presented, to buy into the energy would have not done any good for either of us, and I would have been far from my truth in that moment.

We talked some more, I explained what I would do while I was here. I was being true to myself. He could feel it. I was not kidding. I was serious and this was happening. It was scary for me too, just dropping everything to follow my heart and soul, letting the logical mind take the back seat, and going with my gut. I held strong that feeling and it all worked out just fine.

My Dad really did understand. It was just his own fears of losing me, which was never ever going to happen. He had to let go as well and just accept what was happening. I know he was stressed at the time, so me not being around was a bit of a blow. However, at the end of the day, a parent is really concerned with the happiness of their child, and this was the action at the time I needed to take.

The sheer fact that I was to stay three months and really embrace this time started to excite me no end. It was a good plan and a foundation that I needed to take for the next step of the journey.

Once I knew I was to stay, I took care of all the necessary paperwork for my leave from school. My classes were taken care of. Someone was getting a term of teaching which was opening up a flow for them, and I am doing the one thing that is bringing so much joy to me.

I really knew in my heart that this was the correct thing to do, the best thing at the time, there was no other option. It was like God whispered in my ear,

"You are staying and that's final."

Everything flowed forward from that point. I stayed longer in Maui and I paddled and trained with the Wailea Canoe Club in Kihei. The mornings were beautiful and the waters were calm.

So refreshing to paddle on the deep clear blue ocean and rather comforting to see Haleakala in the distance, It was here on Maui I became friends with the wind 'Makani." Mid morning

I would watch the wind line approaching the shore and it never seemed to drop off until evening.

On one particular day we raced in the wildest and windiest conditions I have ever experienced. It is one of my top five memorable races. (By the way, this is a good question to pose to a long time paddler. There will be some pondering and then they will always come up with interesting stories and adventures.) It was an out and back race, partly with the wind, and then the other half punching into it. Our crew was definitely the most connected on that day. Our purpose and intention for that race was clear and strong.

One of the girls on our team was due to go to the mainland the next week for chemotherapy. She was well enough to race, but some were saying it could be her last, so with that in the back of our minds, we wanted to make it special and memorable for her, and we did just that by crossing the finish line first. It was truly a beautiful gift. The ocean and wind worked with us well.

CHAPTER 19

Big Island

E arly September of 2003, we were to compete in the Queen
Liliu'okalani race in Kona, the first time back to the Big
Island after I had been recognized five years before. Michele one
of my team mates had suggested we go a couple of days early so
we could have a look around. I was keen to do this and she was
also booked in to see her astrologer who was also a clairvoyant.

I was a little apprehensive when she suggested I see her too,
but when I met her, I felt a lot more at ease and decided that it
wouldn't hurt to have a reading. I already knew most of what she
was sharing. It was comforting to get confirmation, and enjoy
a couple of extra perspectives to contemplate from the session.
She asked me if I had anything I wanted to know, and of course I
asked her if she knew if my birth father was alive, and if he lived
in Hawaii?

The answer to that was, yes, he is alive, and he lives in Hawaii.
She was not able to tell me which island, but he was definitely
alive and knew of my existence.

Of course I had some emotion on hearing this and it was
peace of mind to a point, and then more curiosity was stimu-
lated. The other question I asked was which of two Lomi Lomi
trainings was I to attend.

I had signed up for a particular course with one teacher, but
after receiving bodywork from another practitioner and then

hearing he was offering a training too, I was confused as to which one. Now there was choice. This women put my mind at ease, and immediately upon leaving I cancelled the first training and called and booked the other course.

After this visit we continued on down the road with some sight seeing, and felt the energy of the island, especially the volcano at Kilauea. We drove down to the ocean where the lava was flowing. There was such intense heat radiating from the flow, mesmerizing to watch. We were so close to it, such a unique and magical experience, earth growing and forming before our very eyes.

I was so energized, and if someone had said I had to run a marathon right now, I would not have hesitated. Imagine that potential energy waiting to be used. We ended up running out from the lava field back to the car! I felt so alive and energized. The Big Island was very grounding for me.

The race the next day was from Kona to Honaunau, the City of Refuge. The ocean conditions were flat and hot, and the water a brilliant array of blues, absolutely breath taking.

No win on this day for us. However it was the record for the hottest conditions I had experienced. Muscle cramps made their presence felt and I learnt about the importance of magnesium supplementation and prepping the body for racing in the heat. Crazy stuff.

CHAPTER 20

Catalina

The next race of the summer took me to California. The Catalina Crossing was from Newport Beach to Catalina Island. I felt vibrant and strong. I was in Lomi Lomi massage training during the week and for four consecutive days we would be giving and receiving massage with our classmates. I learnt the Hawaiian healing tradition and philosophy, which seemed very familiar to me. I had no conscious reason why.

When it came time to paddle the race, I was so ready to rock and roll. I was a vessel for the energy. Thank goodness I could channel it into the boat. I felt strong and connected.

There were some very accomplished paddlers in the crew, and we all clicked together well for a team that had not practiced before. It was also a mixed team of men and women. The dynamics of the group went well, and we enjoyed paddling in good combinations during the race. The water for the changes was a little bit colder than Hawaii, and quite refreshing.

Our team was styling this weekend, with a beautiful big escort boat and a smaller inflatable which we would do the drops for the changes during the race. We had a chiropractor on board, that was a first for me, and a fabulous sound system on the boat. It was a traveling party on water. I had never been to Catalina Island and I had no idea what it looked like. I was paddling into the unknown. A bit like my life at that point! As mountains and the marina of the island came into view, I was very excited to paddle to a new land. I couldn't help but think of how the early explorers must have felt when they reached the shore of a new destination. Excited, relieved, and ready for adventure. This day turned out well for us. We arrived in first place and won the mixed division and in true outrigger form, it was time to celebrate.

Catalina Island was a little piece of Europe for me, a cosmopolitan feel with gorgeous cobblestone streets, quaint boutiques, plenty of restaurants and of course all the beautiful boats in the marina. I am sure there were some boats that would rival the Monte Carlo marina in the south of France!

The party came after the presentations, and as much fun as it was, I found my self taking a moment away from the crowd. It was a big week, coming from Lomi training and my own internal shifts plus the travel and a four hour race. It was time to stop for a second and integrate.

This is something that comes natural to me, however I didn't always understand my time on my own and sometimes wondered if that was a negative trait of mine. I now know that being a little unsociable is one way to look at it, but I realize its a huge expression of self love and really perfect. We do need to take the time to allow all experience to be integrated. There was more going on for me than I knew.

Sometimes I found it confusing to be with so many people at once, and to just be aware of one's self takes a little pressure off the multitude of energies being experienced at any one time. Certainly being part of any team and even a workplace, family, relationship, there are dynamics playing out and for anyone who is sensitive. They will need a little longer to decipher what is being felt. I found it very important to have the down time to regroup.

I was opening up more. The massage work I was doing was stimulating my abilities and the healer within. Perception, intuition and feelings were heightened. It was interesting to be able to tap into that area, the place that you cannot see but you can feel. I was open and allowing myself to be available for something far greater, a universal force,

God, energy, what ever you want to call it. It was being in the flow so to speak, no coincidences, synchronistic events and meetings and an overall knowing that I am in the right place at the right time. The people I needed to connect with were all being divinely placed in front of me.

Once you decide something, with your heart, it will unfold. Being conscious enough to be able to see it, is the miracle.

I know that everything happens for a reason, but even more powerful is that with our intention, we become the creator of our reality. If we look back on what has happened, all the events will all have a thread that weaves them together. Some will be more significant than others, and others will be experienced to get us into a particular state or feeling that will allow the next pertinent event to occur.

There was a particular meeting with a couple of guys on the plane back to Maui. They had been all over the country presenting seminars about light and healing. I resonated very strongly with them and we talked for most of the flight. One of the guys was an author, his book titled "Wisdom from an Empty Mind." He signed a copy and gave it to me as gift. On the inside cover he wrote, "Robyn, You're a wonderful blend of strength and softness, Don't Change a thing..."

This was such a profound message for me at this time, he was acknowledging me, and he knew who I was already. I was still in the unfoldment. We ended up visiting his home up country in Kula for dinner that week. It was truly exquisite, and from an energy point of view, his house was very clear, clean, and fresh. To have that reflected back at me is quite interesting. There was no clutter, but also being on the slope of Haleakala was pure magic in itself. It was such an inspiring space for me to be in, and I remember that feeling to this day and take that into my own world when I am creating sacred spaces.

The rest of my time in Hawaii was spent training with the Wailea girls on Maui. Then the week leading into the Molokai race, I was back on Oahu with Paula, mostly paddling surf ski and doing my own training. I really threw myself into physical practice. I had taken steps to seek my roots, but paddling was how I was spending my time. I loved to use my body and was fascinated with the whole training, racing experience.

CHAPTER 21

Gold Coast...

After the Molokai race was done, our team disbanded and I flew to Australia that night. A six hour grueling paddle race is not the best preparation for a ten hour flight. It was the end of an incredible summer. I was ready to go home.

The travel worked out perfectly. I flew into Auckland, and then Brisbane. A one hour drive south and I was back on the Gold Coast, happy to be see my Mum and Dad, who were absolutely thrilled to have me home. My sister Roz had made a welcome home sign with my nephew and it was hanging up at the house. She is so thoughtful and the little things like that warm the heart. It was nice to come home to familiar surrounds. It had been a big trip, much transformation and so many wonderful experiences. I was recharged and satisfied for the time being, gently grooved back into my routine of teaching, and had just started practicing yoga in my spare time.

My first yoga class was in Hawaii with Paula and Sarah. It was with Rupali at Yoga Hawaii, in Kaimuki. I really enjoyed it, so once I got back on the coast I found a studio and started attending a few classes a week. I was enjoying the change of pace, the noncompetitive nature and definitely the spiritual aspect of the practice. I loved how I felt when I finished, my mind calm, relaxed and my body limber.

During the days, I was on the water coaching the kids, in the computer room, out on the oval for PE and doing my best at teaching Social Science. There were the odd substitute classes of dance, manual arts and home economics. The students were inspiring. I really enjoyed spending time with them, I wasn't a fan for the institution of school, I found it difficult to be there at times.

I did my work well, but sometimes I was so sensitive, and felt so much when I was at the school, I couldn't wait to get out of that environment. Even though I felt a little constrain I was grateful for having one of the best jobs there and got to be on the water several times a week. I worked along side a talented group of teachers, especially in the Sports Excellence Department and it was motivating being part of a team and making a difference in the students lives. The kids were doing their part too.

I was in the system yet not in the system. I never did think like most, the planning, the finances, marriage. It was like I was in another groove, doing my own thing, walking to the beat of spirit and being guided to do and to not do certain things. I was massaging on my off days as well as helping my parents with chores and errands.

Living with Mum and Dad was a little different after being out of home for many years. I feel so fortunate that I got to spend time with both my parents. I think my Dad was wondering what the hell I was doing. He was looking at me with worry and knew that my mindset was a little different to his. We often butted heads on subjects but there was the utmost respect and love for one another. My mum was going with the flow and always kept an open mind, she had her own health challenges.

CHAPTER 22

Tahiti...

M y sister Roz was busy planning another trip, for which she was very keen to have me be part of. It was the Hawaiki Nui Va'a race in Tahiti. I was not really keen, to tell the truth, mainly because I had just been in Hawaii for three months and couldn't justify spending more money on airfare and accommodation. I must admit, I was feeling how excited she was about it all and the thought of another adventure was appealing to me. I managed to rally, and next thing I knew, I was preparing for another race.

Four years ago, I went to Tahiti for the same race and unfortunately it was a logistical nightmare. I had to clear memory of all that before returning.

The team assembling was from different areas. Bringing all these people together was a massive effort. Girls from Hawaii, California, New Zealand, Sydney, and the Gold and Sunshine Coasts.

We were a group of 12, and we stayed on two yachts for 8 days. What an adventure. Beautiful setting, floating on a spectrum of blue, aqua, turquoise, indigo, and the water was 'light'

The race was not one my better races. However it was a good time being out on the water. It's so beautiful to paddle there, the different color blues are mind blowing!

We sailed to Bora Bora after the racing was done, and that was my very first time with the motor off and the sails hoisted. We were being moved swiftly along by the wind, what an incredible feeling. I spent a great deal of time at the bow of the boat. The feeling of freedom and observing movement across the ocean is captivating to say the least.

For the most part, my time in Tahiti was wonderful, so much beauty to take in and enjoy. However, towards the end of the trip, I had a frightening experience which gave me new appreciation for my eyesight and vision.

We were on the boat celebrating, I had a bottle of champagne, which rarely I drink let alone open the bottles. Being in confined space on the boat, I had the bottle a little too close and the cap exploded and hit my right eye. Holy dooley, that was a shock to the system. Everyone sighed really loud and I instinctively held my eye and simultaneously put my hand up signaling to them to be silent for me in that moment. It was an automatic response, I needed complete silence to just be still and not react for the body. It was very painful but in the moment I had to stop time, and just be in it, and be with it.

After what seemed like a long time, yet only thirty seconds, someone brought me ice to put on it and then all I wanted to do was go and be up on deck in the quiet of the night.

Before going up, I tried to open my eyes to see if I could see. The fear of not being able to, crossed my mind, but I was moving along without much reaction, no judgement, allowing and tending to what needed to be done. Thank heavens I could see. A little scratchy and red, also a small throbbing sensation. After I was checked over, I went up on the deck, sat in the warm breeze, and allowed my bodies response to occur.

The tears came then, in the solitude. I was being gentle with my self, just witnessing my body, and deeply acknowledging and allowing the pain to express and release through my tears.

In hindsight, I was consciously choosing the way to deal with this traumatic experience.

Did I want drama, and to really play out the pain, or did I just want to acknowledge, take care, and be still with it? The latter was my way of handling it.

I went down to my cabin to sleep, I had a piece of hematite stone with me on the trip exactly the size of my eye socket. I needed weight on the eye ball, just a little pressure. The stone was the perfect fit, it was healing and cool to touch, so I put it on my eye and slept with it there the whole night, praying it would do the trick.

The next morning I woke and my eye was a little red but not bloodshot or anything like we thought it might be. There was a little throbbing but it was okay. I swam the next morning, all was fine, but I had to be careful of the salt and the stinging.

I realized how much my gemstones and crystals have been part of my journey and comforting to me. I usually have them on me, either as jewelry or small pocket pieces. We are so blessed for the healing power of our mind, our body and of nature's helpers, in this case my little piece of hematite.

CHAPTER 23

A Space of my Own...

I was so happy to be finally home after being so long away, I was back living with Mum and Dad and had routine. Mornings I paddled kayak, taught school during the day and practiced yoga a few nights a week.

After the races of 2003 in Hawaii and Tahiti, I eventually found myself coaching the women's outrigger team at Surfers Paradise. I paddled a little with a mixed crew which was fun, but it was time for me to change it up, with more emphasis on giving back through the coaching.

From a competitor's point of view, I found I was getting bored. It was time to tread a different path. I felt accomplished and quiet done with that side of me, but I was excited to share what I had learnt over the years and pass on to the new paddlers in the club. So coaching was the natural progression.

I was also immersed in healing work. Being initiated into Reiki levels 1 and II really gave me another perspective of the world I was living in. I became a conduit for more energy or life force. The awareness increased and so did my massage and bodywork schedule. The healing wasn't coming from "me." It was coming through me. Along with my intention, I was the vessel letting this energy be assistance to others. We are ALL capable of this, and the Reiki initiations I had somewhat accelerated this process.

On the subject of health and healing my father was not doing so well at this time. He had his fair share of health challenges and most of 2004 was being close by for him and mum. Despite the discomfort, he kept a sense of humor during much physical pain and suffering.

Illness can take a toll on a person's mind. Much to his credit, it certainly did not interfere with his tremendous foresight and vision.

He was successful at being able to see ahead when it came to property investment. He was the guy who would be one of the first to buy in the areas that would eventually boom.

For instance, he built one of the first commercial factory units in Kortum Drive, Burleigh Heads, which since became a very popular sought after industrial address. He did the same in Machinery Drive Tweed Heads on prime commercial land, also one of the first factory units built. His skill in property investment was very attuned. He definitely had a sixth sense in this area.

With that said and because I was still living at home, we started talking about my next move. There was money in the bank from the sale of properties I had shared with my former partner so buying a place seemed like the way to go. My dad, who had been pondering ideas in his comfy lounge chair said to me with a glint in his eye, "You know what would be ideal?" Right then I knew he was about to share a download on the topic at hand. He then went on to mention a street name, not too far from where they lived. He painted a description of the location, and I could feel that vision and got a sense for that situation. I knew it was going to be light inside and have quite an open feeling. That was my immediate sense.

Well, low and behold, the very next week, we were scanning the newspaper and a unit was for sale in the street he mentioned.

Immediately I got a feeling and I think he knew as well. This was worth a look. I rang the realtor and went there to meet them with the half hour. It was a walk up 2 bedroom unit on the second floor in a block of 6. It was also on the water.

I walked into the place. It was terrible carpet and smelled very smoky but I looked out to the deck onto a wide open water way. I got the feeling straight away that this was my new place. It was plain as day. A couple were interested in it and myself. I didn't even know if I could get the finance for it, but I knew it was the place. This is how quick things can happen.

That afternoon I found myself signing a contract conditional of finance on this unit. It was a bizarre. Here I was sitting at the realtor's desk. My mind couldn't believe it, What was I thinking? I was thinking "Nothing." I was clear in the mind, just following my gut instinct. The Hawaiians refer to this area in the body as the Na'au. I will talk more on this later.

Doubt crept in. I had my moments for sure. When you stay connected and allow for this 'inner knowing' instinct to gather strength through practice on the small things, the body will tell you if its a yay or a nay! It was a yay, and I had to follow that.

My dad couldn't even get up the stairs to look inside it, but from my description he thought it was a good move to at least secure it and then wait to see if I could get approval for the loan. I remember how I felt that day, a little fearful, plenty of nerves, yet an inner knowing of it being the right course of action. This part I was required to trust. This was to be my new home.

The loan was approved, and the property settled on Valentine's Day, 2004. I had a place of my own to call home.

It needed plenty of work, so I got busy, cleaning, painting and cleansing the place of the previous tenants' energy, burning sage and making sure I was satisfied before I spent my first night there. It was sacred ritual for me preparing the space and getting ready to move in. My dear friend Aaron, who I lived with for a little while, helped me move my furniture and got it set up.

It was in an ideal location, right on the water. I could paddle my boat from home to training, which was about a ten minute paddle and there was a small shopping complex across the road with a bakery, groceries and even a restaurant. It was walking distance to my parents' house and the nearby sports complex and only a ten minute walk to the beach.

The time I was there was really fun. I enjoyed entertaining, cooking for friends, afternoon drinks on the lanai, and yoga practice in the living room.

The two days I was not teaching at the school I was massaging clients, and it was a very relaxing location for them as well as convenient.

My parents finally came over to visit, Dad made it up the stairs successfully and I am so glad he got to see the vision manifested!

I had spare room and ended up having friends come and stay now and again. Due to my involvement with the paddling community, I hosted international athletes who came to the Gold Coast to train, and for three months I rented out the spare room to a married couple from England. These two souls were great to live with. We always enjoyed "putting the kettle on," and I think I drank more tea than ever during their stay. We had great meals and did the occasional social activity together. They were busy with the training. Geof was a sports psychologist and Rachel was working as a radiographer. He was also her paddling coach.

By that time my training was starting to ease off, and I was coaching more and paddling for fun. The intensity of the paddling began to be a little too much for me, and I was practicing more yoga and heading in the opposite direction to competition. It was an interesting contrast with us all living in the same space.

If anything I got to see how I had changed, because I used to do all that physical training, but now, other things captured my interest. It was so lovely to have their company. I wasn't spending a great deal of time elsewhere, and things were still unfolding.

I had made enquiries regarding the adoption and information, but for some reason, I kept hitting brick walls, I don't think it was the time for it to open up. The universe has a divine schedule for everything as I have come to learn.

CHAPTER 24

Divine Intervention...

Probably about mid year 2004 I was running some errands and was in the Post Office at Miami, on the Gold Coast. I happened to run into Miles who was the son of my Dad's best fishing mate, Joe. My dad and Joe had many years of friendship, and they loved to fish together, on the beach and out on the boat. I know for sure Dad wasn't a swimmer and Joe was a better runner than swimmer, so the thought of the two of them out on the water is rather humorous. Joe was our track coach for athletics, a wonderful man, and has since passed on.

I had not seen Miles for quite a while, but what is always refreshing about running into an old family friend is that they have known you since you were little, they know your history, and have watched you grow up. It's really sweet, that feeling of Ohana, our extended family. Miles and I got chatting and he happened to question me regarding adoption. His wife was adopted and he encouraged her to seek out her biological parents. All stories are different, with a variety of motivations, and once they had their own child, it triggered them to go that route. He then asked me if I had ever decided to find my biological parents.

I told Miles that I had taken the first step and that I had been notified of the mothers name but I didn't know where she was and was not sure of the next step. For me it hadn't been the "right time" to pursue. With Dad being ill, it was a bit too much to go completely down that track. I think what I realize in hindsight is once you decide to do something, the universe starts to shuffle things into place, and other people are affected indirectly and directly so I was always conscious of this. We all know it, not wanting to hurt feelings, or step out of line. On a subconscious level, it was probably because I was unable to handle all that energy processing through me at once. That's what I believed at the time, I was very aware of how my parents would feel and they already knew I had a name for the mother but something was guiding me against going full steam ahead. I listened. It was about timing. We are all essentially energy and the vibration of us and our intentions run far and wide! We are listening to our gut, our heart, our Na'au.

After I told Miles, he looked at me and said, "I am glad you are doing that, just don't leave it to long." Certainly, we all have had someone say to us something with such conviction that it appears to be coming from a higher source, like God was talking to me face to face. Well, that's exactly how it felt when he told me that. Everything in that sentence was source energy expressing through the vehicle of another human being. Don't you love it?

Our conversation in the post office was the catalyst I needed to take the next step. Something was woken up in me to take action immediately. So I went home, got on the computer and got the number of the adoption department. I needed to talk to someone about it right in that moment.

The woman I spoke to was very helpful and I asked her what was my next step. We talked a while. It was like a little counseling session I guess. She was going to send me some info and put me in touch with a group. She could also tell me how I could go about finding more information about the birth mother, after all, I had her name now, the next step was finding out through marriage or even death records to see where she was.

A group was not what I was requiring at that particular time. I was sensitive and open as it was.

I had pulled away from group energy just so I could get a little more in tune and in touch with who I was in all this. As much as I was grateful for the suggestion I knew deep down that was never going to happen. Sometimes there is too much of a victim energy. I was not looking at this as being a victim, I loved that someone had brought me in, birthed me, and then others had taken care and given me a life. I was interested in putting my jigsaw together and moving forward. With that decision I made another call and then had a game plan.

The next thing I was to do was to go to the records of marriages and deaths. I got another letter saying who she had married. They even gave me the name of the church she was married in which happened to be walking distance from my house!

Next step was the electoral roll, where you can get the information for the last known address. This took a few weeks. I was happy to be sharing this with my British flatmates. We conversed regularly and looked at all angles. It was helpful with Geoff being a psychologist because he was able to give me questions that would give different viewpoints and allow me to open to wider perspective. I did not wish to burden my family with all this. It didn't feel right. It was something I was wanting to find out so, I just went ahead and did it.

A crazy thing happened whilst in the electoral office in Southport. I had her husbands name now and was able to get a printout of her address.

Guess where the address was? It was literally the house across the road where my dad's friend Joe used to live and now his son Miles and his wife and family live. I was blown away.

This was too uncanny. Miles was the very one who said to me in the Miami post office to not leave it too long. Wow, and here he is living across the road from my biological mother!

I was in total shock. I had to tell Miles. He gave me his card that day in the post office a month or two before.

CHAPTER 25

Contact...

Wow, so close to home, within a two mile radius of where I have lived, gone to school, run, walked, swam in the local pool, gone to the shopping center and the beach. It was a surprise and I think I may have told my sister and Erin first, Erin spent time with Miles years back and is one of my sisters best friends. She is a big time public relations and marketing wizard in tourism and travels all over the globe with the companies she has worked for. I have paddled with her many years in the canoe, and all of us were always so proud of her and her career travels. It was exciting for everyone that she was getting to go to these very interesting places throughout the Pacific, Asia, and even the Middle East with her career. I knew she would be surprised and might even have a little information of the neighbors in the area, maybe she knew indirectly who my biological mother was? Maybe she has waved to her, smiled or even spoken to her out and about in the street?

Erin was very surprised, as was my sister. There was much going on that particular day in our paddling community. We were having a little send off ceremony for one of our fellow paddlers who had tragically died a couple of weeks earlier. Our girls crews arranged to do a memorial paddle from The Alley at Currumbin. This was a very strange time, so many different things happening and now this. We took part in a beautiful ceremony from the point, reminiscing on the attributes of this bright being who we all had the pleasure and joy of paddling with over the last couple of years.

I remember walking along the beach back to where the boats were, I think we paddled back into the estuary to where we initially launched from, and then it was over to a waterfront cafe for some lunch. I couldn't hold it in any longer. We finally farewelled our teammate, and within the next half hour I asked Erin if she had ever known of a woman named Astrid, who lived across the road from Miles. Erin vaguely recalled the neighbors and said that there was a "Polish" women who lived across the road who was always out in the garden.

Oh my god! My heart was absolutely racing. Curiosity was building rapidly, and then I told her, that possibly this "Polish" women is my birth mother!

After dropping that bombshell, Erin was desperately searching her mind, trying to recall anything and everything of those times where she may have seen the woman in the garden or even heard her speak. The one thing she did recall about her, is that she was always very friendly.

It was good to hear that!

Okay, take a deep breath everyone....

There happened to be another women paddling for the club who I have coached in the masters' program. She's a lovely person and lives a few doors down from Miles.

I knew she had lived in this street because I had been to her house once before, about 2 years prior. Di was a teacher, and back then she got me some temporary work at an International School. In the mornings we were in the classroom teaching English to Japanese students, and the afternoons were out and about, taking them on excursion to the various tourist attractions. Another seemingly innocent unrelated connection, but inadvertently on some level she was leading me back or at least to the energetic vicinity of my biological roots. It's amazing when I trace back that everything is linked.

"Oh yes, of course, I know Astrid. She's that lovely woman who comes door knocking each year for the Red Cross," said Di. Oh my goodness, by now I was just thinking, this is so bizarre.

First she lives across the road from my Dad's best friends son, then a woman who I have been involved with in my outrigger canoe club knows and has spoken to her every year for several years. She knows about her wonderful garden. I shake my head in amazement.

Without detracting from the reason we were all gathering we quietly faded that conversation out and I was assimilating all I had heard. When we finished lunch and went our separate ways, I pulled Miles's card out of my wallet and called him from the parking lot of the cafe.

He was happily surprised to hear my voice, and I told him of my new information. I gave him the street number and he confirmed that was the house across the road from him. I asked if he knew Astrid. He said, "yes, of course, she's the Polish woman who is always in the garden." I replied back to him. "That Polish women just happens to be my birth mother."

"You're kidding," he said. "No way"

"I am not kidding," I truthfully replied.

He was in complete shock.

Finally he composed himself and started to share every detail he could recall. He knew how important this was to me. Every little piece of info helps make up the puzzle. He told me that she has since left the house because her husband was ill so they moved into a unit somewhere, but he wasn't sure exactly where but would find out for me. I asked him to do it discreetly as I was not ready for full disclosure and it might be a little bit of a shock after thirty-four years, who knows what the response would be? Things were now speeding up. I knew this would happen and I think that's why we take our time with things, then the divine steps in to monitor our readiness and progress.

I was so blown away with how all the pieces are starting to fall into place.

Miles was very excited for me and was very helpful in this part of the process. Within twenty-four hours I had the name, address and phone number. When you really want something to happen, it happens quickly. I wonder if the slower we are with our process, we are purposely savoring the moments, enjoying the pose, to coin a yogic expression. It also can be a place of safety, comfort and control of circumstances. I believe it is an 'energy' thing, In my own words it's kind of like this -

> *Once you open the door, you have to be ready to*
> *receive the energy and to be able to transmute,*
> *discern and just be present in what is happening.*
> *There is the knowing that you have had all*
> *along within, then there is the unfolding.*
> *In hindsight, I believe we have a*
> *silent hand in writing the script.*
> *That might be a little way out there, but*
> *then again, I know there will be some*
> *of you who will resonate with this.*

Miles discovered that Astrid's husband had passed a few months ago.

They had moved from the house into a waterfront unit at Mermaid Waters, where she was able to look after him better. A relative living in the house gave this information to Miles without any fuss. How easy was that? So I have all this information.

What was the next step? Just call her up? No, not likely. I was happy to find this out, but it was not in an official way. I had the part of me that wanted to go about it "officially."

Something in me was telling me to go about it with a little more officialdom, I did not want to put Miles in the middle, so I went back to the electoral office and confirmed that information.

At least then I could say I received it from official sources. At the time I felt happier about this.

As I write, I am having very interesting insights of the type of person I have been, the good girl, likes to do the right thing in the right way. I am happy to have options to get things done, or to make things happen, and for the record I am open and a little more free in my approach to have things occur divinely and trusting in the way they arrive. But nothing wrong with a little confirmation to ease the construct of the mind!

Next question. How do I make contact? I certainly was not ready to call, that would just be too full on at this point. A letter would be my best form of communication to start with.

I had an air of detachment about me, I have come this far and have been helped every step of the way. I was aware of my parents, my sister, the feelings of the people around me, was I aware of my own feelings? What was I going to feel? Would I change? Would I like her? Would she even want to contact me? All the uncertainties of the mind, came racing in, but my attitude was curiosity. If she is open then great, if she is not, then it's not meant to be.

With all this in consideration I started to pen the letter. Screwing the paper quite a few times, getting frustrated, then leaving it for a little while.

My sister and I did a drive by of where she lived. By this time Rozi was excited for me, and all my negative thoughts of how she might feel were thrown away, she was very supportive and I was so blessed to have her understanding. I could at least share this part with her. We were like little school girls driving down the street secretly pointing at the house, wondering if we may catch a glimpse, but luckily not this time. It was for the pure joy and fun of discovery.

What was even more crazy, was that it was on the water, and it was just near the 2Km mark on our paddling course, I used to paddle my kayak in training past this house EVERY day. Sometimes twice a day. Can you believe it?

The story was getting more woven, many threads intersecting now, all those sessions on the water, the times where I would be running out of breath at about that point where her house was.

I distinctly remember during some sessions, at that particular place on the canal, I just wanted to throw it all away, literally. My body would be tired and unknowingly I was so close to the answer of my big question!

CHAPTER 26

Watery Wisdom...

Some days, I would get on the water and in the warm up I would just cry and release, thinking I was crazy for feeling so deeply and not understanding what was going on. I had so much "energy in motion" (emotion) moving through me at times it was overwhelming, and I would be crying and just letting go each time I paddled. My astrological sign is Cancer and my dominant element is WATER! It figures, right?

At the time it was the only place I felt like I was at home. Water is so nurturing, and I guess it is like the osmosis effect, the water in me, or the emotion just wanted to come out and join the big body of water. That's its nature, and I am sure I could speak for many on this.

Feeling and being sensitive can be looked at as a curse or as a gift. I was much in the former place for a little while, with my logical mind trying to figure it all out, get spiritual, cleanse, whatever it took. Paddling was more of a retreat, a spiritual experience, a place to connect with God or something bigger. Kept me expansive and feeling connected. My soul is so happy being on the water.

I was living and feeling my way through all areas of my life. My work, my seeking, my relationships. My mind was not working for me at all in the sense that if I was to compare with the people around me, I don't even think I knew how to use it without trusting it. I really believe, all my experiences to that point were to prepare me, to receive, to trust the divine guidance, have it reconfirmed and accept who I am by feeling my way home.

I am deep, I feel, I always have, I always will and this was part of the journey to understand more of who I was, the biological parents, the story, and how life has unfolded thus far. The paddling defined me to a point, the training, the racing the coaching, but it was in the feeling, the connection, the essence of balance where I was open for something greater to express through me.

I did however get tired of being this energy muse, transmuting and losing myself in this. I believe on a level I put myself in this life to experience so much, that sometimes I would not know where I started or ended.

The paddling allowed me to connect with my true self, the breath, the moment and the water was being the conductor. The body was in complete balance sitting in the boat. If you have ever tried to paddle or even sit in a K1 Olympic race kayak, you will quickly know if you are not connected and present or not, then you will fall in. It's a practice. Rarely does someone just get in and paddle fast without falling in the drink.

Discipline in whatever the practice, building neuromuscular pathways to remember the connection, leads to the freedom. An analogy for life.
"I bless that body of water with all my heart for sustaining me and guiding me, if water is an entity and energetically alive, then that canal system knew me well, my story and my soul."

As this part of my search was coming to completion, my need to be on that water dwindled, it was tiring to go back, over the same currents, day in, day out.

The water brought all things to me, and the discipline of that physical training definitely brought me freedom of spirit and truth.

CHAPTER 27

Open to Grace...

I often reflect on the gratitude for this whole experience, for my spiritual awakening, my healing, and the path that started ten years prior. If I wasn't paddling and trying to be the best I could be, then the body work, the emotional clearing, the understanding of who I am in the larger sense and the detachment necessary to take this to another level with love would not have happened.

To go this route, it was necessary to play this way. To come from a higher perspective, without victim consciousness, to know, to heal, and to love. My intention was a win win situation for everyone involved. I needed to know and have a clear path, for my future, for my future partner, my children, and their children, it was my kuleana (responsibility) to Self to embark on this journey.

I had the information and was just waiting for the letter to come through me. I was so curious, I wanted to find my roots. I shared with my family the information of where Astrid lived and of her husband's occupation. It seemed my dad knew of him through the real estate circles.

The flow was open. I wrote during the day in my unit. A pile of scrap paper and scribble for the most part, but finally I was happy with what I wrote. I needed some objective feedback so I called a woman who was also in the outrigger club. She was very open and gifted psychically. It was interesting that I went to her, she was the first person I thought of for this kind of thing. Unrelated, no judgement, no interest, just honest opinion, with a little more intuition on her side.

I didn't want to sign my last name at this point, that would be divulging too much information and I was considering my family as well. There would be plenty of time for that. My friend agreed and she said, "Your letter is neutral. It is to the point, non threatening, with no expectation."

I was happy with the draft and then finally put it in the post. The other good thing is that I had a post box number at the time, so no address. It was quiet interesting I had wanted to keep privacy at this point and was not ready to divulge certain information. I noticed I was rather protective of my self and my family. It was a natural response. Maybe others might be different in this situation, but I honored what I was feeling and moved at my own pace.

That was a load off my chest. It's out there now. I was not attached to the outcome. Unconditionally, I opened to grace.

Copy of letter (for privacy I have deleted surname)

PO Box 298
NOBBY BEACH
Qld 4218

21 September 2004

Dear Astrid
My name is Robyn and I was born as Louisa _____ on 2nd July
1968, in Brisbane.
I am 36 years of age. I have been doing a search for my birth parents
and that is why you are receiving this mail.

My birthmother was listed on the original birth certificate as
Astrid _____born in Surabaya, Indonesia, and from my search
information I have reason to believe that this could be you.

I realise this may come as a surprise or shock, so take whatever time
you need to process this, I have had to do the same.

I have no idea how you may feel about me contacting you, but for
me I would like to put my jigsaw puzzle pieces together. It would
be nice to know who my birth parents were, where they were from,
(my heritage in particular) and maybe a possibility of meet one day
if you agree to. I would like to hear you story sometime, and how I
came to be.

I am of open mind. I am sure it would put both of us at peace. I will
not contact you by phone unless you say it is ok to do so.

I would be more than happy to exchange letters for a while if you
wish.

Obviously we may both have had our own emotion wrapped
around this part of us, however at the end of the day, it could be a
good thing to clear and just chat. I would like this to happen at the
least.

Yours truly,

CHAPTER 28

A Speedy Reply....

There it was, in my mailbox, the very next day. Handwritten, with a return address on the back. It was Astrid! My heart was racing. The envelope was quite thick, inside was going to be something to surprise me, I was excited with much anticipation. I decided to go somewhere special to read it, so I went to Pizzey Park, the sporting complex my Dad helped develop and raised funds for. They named it after him too. It was the perfect place.

There was a grassy spot with a table in the shade and by the lake so that was my spot. It was a place that had given me much comfort, much activity and fun times. There was plenty of space, and no one about, a little nature haven in suburbia. The fact I was in my Dad's park allowed me to feel rooted and steady, for what I was about to read was to confirm what I felt and knew within.

It was a neatly written letter expressing how excited and happy she was to hear from me, there was a little background information about her husband's recent death, that her mother and step brother were visiting at the moment from Denmark and then there it was in writing, on the last page and towards the end of the letter.....

"I was looking after 7 kids in Hawaii when I met your father, who took my mother who was visiting me, and myself to Greens Sands Beach, which one can only get to by walking or by four wheel drive."

CHAPTER 29

Confirmation

Seeing the word "Hawaii" written, I had this well of emotion and tears started to stream from my eyes. It was something I had an inkling of, that I knew and felt it in my heart and it all made sense.

From my studies of Lomi Lomi, the Hawaiian culture, the deep spirituality, and connectedness with nature, the Hawaiian in me was acknowledged in a couple of lines of this letter. Just seeing the word 'Hawaii' in print had me bawling.

I wasn't even sure in my mind but something else in my body, in my being, was registering. All my time in the islands, knowing something but not knowing for sure, searching for the unknown parts of me, just to see it written was enough to stimulate and stir the depths of my soul. A little more of the jigsaw puzzle was being put into place.

I remember feeling very much alone on this path, and sometimes, that is exactly what is required to reach the places deep within, to reach your true Self, the divine knowing within. Our true connection to spirit.

"Alone" is not necessarily to be lonely
It is an opportunity to be
"ALL ONE"

Astrid had not told any of her family of my existence and finished the letter by saying she had no idea how she was going to break the news to her mother. I can't imagine.

When I read this letter some seven years later, it is not much different from the many, many letters I have received since, it is rather cute and there is a real openness in her writing expression, that I love. The words come to life and the descriptions are very animated and very expressive, a wonderful way to share her experiences.

So here I was in the park, tears and all, no one around but the birds witnessing this moment. Feeling somewhat different yet the same, not really knowing what to do next, thank goodness for the breeze, the trees, the water in the lake and the ducks floating around in front of me. It was a very comforting place for me. There was stillness and truth reflecting itself back to me and permeating the space. I rested in that place for sometime.

Fortunately, I did not have the 9-5 Monday to Friday gig. My work was part-time and there was no way this would ever have happened the way it did had I been in a strict routine. I know that everything happens for a reason. I also know that we create our experiences. We are the dreamer of the dream, and for this to unfold the way it did, all happened in divine right order.

Walking back to my car I was experiencing many different feelings. I felt excited, scared, happy and joyful all at once. I really wanted to share with my parents for the pure joy of discovery, but I was not sure how they would react. I decided to tell them anyway without any fears or other things attached to it. I prayed they would receive this news well and in good stead.

From Pizzey Park I drove a couple of minutes up the road to my parents' house.

I think my Mum was happy, my Dad remained aloof, listening but not really and then kind of moving on. I tried not to take this personal as I know how he was feeling. We were very much alike. Our issues get triggered at certain times and the "abandonment" thing was very much in our faces. I knew that he would take a little warming to the idea, but I didn't push it.

I was just happy to be honest and be able to share the news. I was in my truth.

With that done, I decided to let it unfold naturally and share when I felt. Dad had other things going on that he was dealing with so I had no need to compound the issue. Of course the best scenario is when people can really celebrate your good news with you, your wins. I have learnt that it's very important where and when you share. It's an energy exchange. There is no point in wasting your energy talking to a brick wall or into a space that is unreceptive to your communication. I was also aware that he was mirroring my own hesitation, so I was thankful for that higher perspective and point of view.

Once you go ahead with a process like this, the unravelling of emotion and energy starts. Not just you, but for the other people involved as well. The ripple effect...

CHAPTER 30

I respond...

The letter was very informative, just like she was chatting to me, so I felt a little more at ease and thrilled for the positive response. I remember feeling very protective and not wanting to divulge so much. Maybe it was a little fear or something else surfacing. It was quite a weird feeling, talking about my self to my birthmother who did not even know who I was.

I intended this experience to be harmonious and healing, and was not interested in playing any of the other stuff that may come up in these situations. I knew there was good reason for being put up for adoption, I was curious to find this out and also wondering what was happening for her at the time and how she felt.

After I got info about her whereabouts, I had a conversation with the adoption people, they sent me this little brochure about the emotions and the common issues of abandonment, resentment, anger, all this stuff from the perspective of the adoptee, the birth parents and the adoptive parents, so many angles. I wondered what it was all about. Do I have to go down that road?

Respectfully, and lovingly I went my own path.

> *When you start clearing your emotional baggage, it allows you to be much more present and the triggers are not in place any more.*

*Something may happen to you, but it
doesn't provoke a subconscious reaction.
You have opportunity to consciously
choose how you wish to react.
You are not free from feeling. You just
don't have the energetic charge.*

I really felt that my spiritual work, the learnings, the teachings, the experiences, the emotional clearing and my general level of awareness held me in good stead to be present during this experience.

I was in a place to receive and it was intended to be something great, and whatever came up would be dealt with from a higher perspective. I wasn't sure how I felt but I do know I was reluctant to give out too much information too soon. I did have a little stuff around that, but I took my time and then wrote a brief letter telling her a little more about me and my life thus far.

In this type of situation you really are starting from scratch. There's no preconception or anything. I went in open to allow for freedom and healing from both sides, I was totally curious and eager to find out more about her, my ancestry and more information about the father.

I knew this would help me piece my jigsaw puzzle together and give me a little more insight into aspects of myself.

I got a prompt second reply and because I wrote a little about my outrigger paddling, she mentioned something interesting and threw a whole different slant on the picture, which kind of blew me out of the water.

Six degrees of separation and there are NO, I repeat, NO coincidences.

Astrid mentioned in the first letter that she used to look after seven kids in Hawaii.

In this particular letter, she says that one of the boys she used to look after and his wife now are outrigger paddlers in Hawaii. Both have even been to visit her on the Gold Coast after racing at Hamilton Island. "Do you know Tim and Maggie?"

I couldn't believe what I just read. Just a couple of years back, I was at Tim's fortieth birthday party at Diamond Head, meeting and partying with his friends and family, the very same family that my birthmother used to look after thirty-five years ago. It was after that party on my return to Australia that I made the first steps in my search. It was a catalyst certainly, and just being in that environment must have woken my spirit guides hustling me to get a move on and start my search.

At the end of my second letter to her, I put my phone number and was open to be contacted in person. There was much to talk about just with that information shared. Wow! This was getting exciting for me now. I wanted to know more about her life in Hawaii and the mutual connection with this family. Intriguing stuff!

*"We are definitely being guided. There
is another realm at work.
Conspiring to move us in the direction of our dreams.
An orchestra of many players seen and unseen.
We are open minded, listening, following
and learning to trust that guidance.
We are always being guided.
We are being guided even when we are unaware."*

CHAPTER 31

The Big Game

I must say I was very happy to receive the letters, I remember checking my mail before driving to school and even showing it to John who I taught with. He was so happy for me as he knew that I was in that place of seeking more. I was not the happiest at school because there was always a part of me, not wanting to be there. As much as I loved the kids, it just didn't 'feel' right. There was so much going on, I was changing, Dad was suffering, Mum was hanging in there, and my sister was doing her best, busy with work and family. We learn so much from family. It really is the unconditional love that is shared, and acceptance of one another. In our family, we were of many tribes, unrelated by blood, but working and harmonizing as best as we could.

In the most recent letter of this time from Astrid mentioned in her most recent letter that she was going to Brisbane for the weekend, and that she hadn't told her mother about my existence.

She wondered how she was going to do this and would find the right time sometime over the weekend.

It was Sunday night and I was at home having dinner with Rach and Geof. The television was on the football. In Australia, one of the biggest events in Australian sport is the National Rugby League (NRL) Grand final. Most of the nation were glued to the television watching the game.

We were kind of interested but not completely in to it. They were sitting in the living area on my comfy modular couch and I was chopping sweet potato, peeking over every now and again at the game.

The phone ringing brought me out from my chopping trance. I reached over to answer it. I hear this very strong English accent from the woman on the other end of the line.

"Hello Robyn?" My eyebrows lifted in anticipation. "Hello. Is that you Astrid?" "Yes," the woman replied. The first thing that came out of my mouth was "Oh my God, it's you!"

We giggled a little, and it was very matter of fact, like I knew her, and we were talking like old friends, laughing and carrying on.

She told me that her mother was visiting from Denmark, along with her step brother and that they were listening in the background. She also said that she broke the news of my existence to her mother that morning while they were visiting her uncle on Tamborine Mountain, about a 40min drive from the Gold Coast.

I asked Astrid how her mother reacted with the news of me, the first thing she said was, "So, when are we going to meet her?" It sounded like she was absolutely thrilled.

From what my birthmother had said in that recent letter, she had only told one person in Brisbane, and that was the girl I think she was visiting that weekend.

It was interesting to hear also that her younger brother, who lives in New Zealand, adopted a baby girl, twenty or so years ago. That was in different times, a contrast in that all was out in the open. They knew the birth parents and it was a harmonious relationship between all. This was right in front of her the whole time, so it must have been rather difficult for Astrid to hold a secret of my existence.

It's was so bizarre, I have been a secret to some, but not to others. My existence known in one place yet not in another. In her world, I have been only in her mind and heart, as with many children that were for whatever reason adopted out. So many realities were being played out simultaneously.

We probably spoke on the phone for maybe 10 or so minutes, and then she said, "We would love to meet you, when would be a good time?" I was buzzing with much excitement, and the words just fell out of my mouth. "Now, would be a good time."

I hung up and the phone and left the sweet potato on the cutting board. It was time to meet the woman who birthed me.

My roommates, who were still watching the football, could hear our conversation and said later that they thought I was just talking to a friend. When I told them it was my birthmother, they nearly fell off the couch. They motioned me quickly towards the door in their cute British accent. "Go on then, off you go."

Of course, I knew where to go. My sister and I had had already done the drive by,

just a four minute drive away. Her unit was very close to where my partner and I many years before bought our first home.

Driving there, I was a little nervous, maybe a little heart guarded, but at the same time really excited. I drove a little way past the property, turned around and parked on the street in front.

I saw a figure come out the front door and she was walking towards the car. I couldn't quite see her in the dark, but I could feel her smile from where I was, she was totally beaming me!

Here I am about to make physical contact with my birth mother for the first time since she popped me out.

I got out of the car, and walked towards her and I could see her much better.

We embraced with a friendly hug. We were giggling and she was wanting to see what I looked like, as I was too. It felt very natural. There wasn't a big emotional response or tears. It was pure joy and fun. I guess the laughter is a good way to respond to the myriad of emotions we both may have had stored up. It was wonderful to experience such a profound meeting in this light hearted way. There was much anticipation and eagerness to see each other and check each other out.

We both were very happy.

Then came a change of pace. We are physical beings, but essentially we are energy. We vibrate a frequency. Our cells vibrate, mostly at a level that is subtle and we are unaware, unless we are sensitive to energy. Then it's very apparent when something or someone enters our energy field.

I walked through the door and standing there was my paternal grandmother. The Danish affectionately call the grandmother "Mormor," meaning mother's, mother. If it is the grandmother on the fathers side, she is known as "Farmor," or father's mother.

Mormor stood in front of me in a long flowing dress. It was a muumuu dress from Hawaii. She had a very regal grin on her face and her arms opened towards me.

In a strong Danish/English accent she spoke.

"Hello Robyn."

"Welcome to our family."

We hugged and I felt my cells vibrate off the charts, it was so much energy and then the tears started flowing. It was inevitable, I looked more like her, I definitely felt a strong connection, and resonance, it was a big chunk of me right there in that moment. Mormor was a very wise soul, and very deep feeling. I knew this straight away, because that was me. Something clicked right there. I was happy, I felt at home and it was time to celebrate.

Here we are, three generations, all together for the very first time.

Christopher, Astrid's stepbrother, was also visiting from Denmark and witnessing all this. He was great with taking care of us all, holding space and hosting this auspicious gathering. He brought us all a small glass of wine to celebrate with.

We sat down and made a toast to our coming together this night. While the rest of the country were watching football, we were making our own history.

I was still vibrating. It was like my cells were changing. Things were definitely moving inside of me quickly. Something was being awoken. More of my jigsaw pieces were coming together.

We talked story for a few hours, I lead a fairly similar path to my grandmother as she was growing up. She was very active, good at sport, a physical education teacher like I was, so we had a lot in common. Astrid also very active, playing netball in her day like me and swimming. We both loved the outdoors, nature and loved people, and she spent much of her life looking after others.

We were compared body parts, like feet and toes and facial features.

There were a few physical similarities. I also asked my grandmother about when she had her last child, and if there was anything in the family medical history I would need to know, especially, if I was to have a child. She was thirty-nine when pregnant, so that was good to hear.

I had a feeling that would be the case. I have never stressed about my age. I do know as you get older the egg quality apparently decreases, so hearing that she gave birth later in life was peace for my mind. They were both very healthy and active, My grandmother was eighty-nine at the time I met her, she was so thrilled to know that I was her first granddaughter, she had others but they were a lot younger than me.

I asked them about Suryabaya, Indonesia which was on my birth extract, and where Astrid was born. Her father was working there and when the Japanese occupied Indonesia in World War II, the women and children were separated from the men. Mormor lost her husband and her father during this time to illness. Astrid and her brother and my grandmother went to live in England when the war ended, as that is where her husband was from and where they were planning to spend life. Both kids without father, and mother having to make it the best way she could for her children, made for tough times.

Both kids went to boarding school and Mormor eventually remarried and lived in Denmark. One of her other grand daughters wrote a biography of my grandmothers life, which is very interesting. It was incredibly tough times, but her attitude for life is amazing and positive. Adversity tests us all, and thankfully can also bring out the goodness and zest for life, for every day is a blessing.

With questions and questions, just looking in awe at each other, some laughter, some tears, it was an incredibly full evening to say the least.

I had definitely changed after that meeting, I could feel it. Viscerally, I felt different. I felt whole in the sense that my questions were answered. Some of them. Astrid and I had much more to talk to about.

Meeting my Danish grandmother was a kinesthetic experience, it was as if my cells were still doing cartwheels and buzzing with a remembrance. I got to look at people who looked a little like me. This was different, a very new experience for me, not for people who have grown up looking at their biology, the actual flesh and bone. I had never seen that perspective before. I could see and feel how much joy there was for her, and after what she had been through in her life to date, finding out that morning that she had another grand daughter was wonderful uplifting news.

We wound up conversation for the time being and I got ready to head for home. I was excited and simultaneously aware there was integration occurring for each of us. I was in disbelief driving home, in a good way. So long ago, I set the intention to meet her and I just did. It is amazing when it all comes at you, the convergence. That's the part we cannot control or even envision exactly what it will look like when it happens.

I had myself such a unique entry and upbringing in the world. The main thing was that I was taken care of, loved from near and afar and completely blessed to have come full circle, a gift for us all. You can never have too much love.

After a short reflective drive home, I was ready for a much needed sleep and integration. Tomorrow was a brand new day.

I was different. Maybe I could describe it as feeling more grounded, we all shared quite a lot that night and surely our meeting changed us all in some way. Healing occurs and continues to happen. Also it was fun to find things out. I was looking forward to seeing them both again.

I told a couple of my colleagues the next day at school, and they were so happy for me. I told my parents, and they were okay. Mum was great. Dad was still a little unsure of what to make of it all. I understood his feelings. I was honoring my journey sharing when I felt inspired and taking it in my stride, one step at a time.

One afternoon, I paddled my kayak around to Astrid's unit on the water. She had told me that for years she had watched all the paddlers go past her place, she had no idea that I was one of them. We had shopped at the same stores, swam at the same pool, probably crossed paths somewhere over the years. It was great to chat about things and see the areas we had in common, even some of the people we knew mutually, but without anyone, including ourselves, knowing the connection.

Most of my friends knew of my search and were thrilled to hear. Astrid and I would meet every now and again for coffee or lunch, sometimes a walk on the beach. She was really active and we got to talk story on our own. She also continued writing the letters, which was good because I learnt a lot about her through the writings. I felt a little resistance every now and again. I think we both were processing some stuff and we talked about the reason for putting me up for adoption.

It's only human nature that there would be a myriad of feelings both from the mother and the child in this situation. I wished for this to be positive for us both and intended that all would be well and we would remain in each other lives in some capacity. It took a little adjusting. I had hoped that my family would meet her, and I knew this would happen in divine perfect time. My sister was the first to meet Astrid. They of course, hit it off immediately. Rozi has a great sense of humor and Astrid likes to chat and laugh. My nephew Ethan instantly warmed to her. I think he liked her strong English accent because it was different to what he was accustomed to hearing, and with all her years looking after kids, she was a natural with him.

CHAPTER 32

The other half of the mystery....

Next question. What about the father?
I was very curious to hear more on that and if she had any information for me. We talked about this a few visits in. I had many questions for her. Why did she give me up? Who was the father? Is he still alive? Where is he? She was happy to discuss this and told me what she knew up to this day.

My biological father was from a little town called Na'alehu on the Big Island of Hawaii. They had met whilst at South Point, on the Big Island which happens to be the very southern most tip of the USA.

Her mother had asked him for a ride into to Green Sands Beach, which was a couple of mile in and only accessible by walking or four wheel drive. He happily drove them in on the bumpy coastline trail. The beach is named Green Sands because the sand has tiny specs and pieces of olivine (peridot) in it.

After that initial meeting, they struck up a friendship and then started to see one another here and there. He liked to dive, and loved to fish, and loved the solitude of the South Point area. It is an energy vortex and when you visit there, it definitely has a certain unique feel to it.

One thing obviously led to another between them, and the next thing you know I was in the womb! When Astrid became pregnant, she told only one friend in Kona and then continued to work for the family in Hilo, but would soon be starting to show. She had so many decisions to make. She didn't tell him until after I was born. She said she wasn't in love with him and couldn't envision staying, so hence made the decision to have me in Brisbane, Australia.

She wanted the best for me and at the time, adoption was a viable option. I feel for her not being able to share this. Who is to judge, really, that is not useful nor the point. I am so happy and blessed to be here and have an amazing life.

Astrid left Hawaii prematurely, on a boat bound for Australia. It was 6 weeks I believe that she was at sea pregnant with me. Maybe that's one of the many reasons I love the ocean so much!

CHAPTER 33

More questions....

S he did write to my birthfather once I was born and told him the news. He replied with "Why didn't you stay? We could have had a great life together." He had a family already, his wife had passed away before they met.

I trust that her decision was in my best interest as hard as it was for her to adopt me out. She really wanted me to be raised with both a mother and a father and to give me the best opportunity in life which she at the time was unable to provide. She didn't have a father around her growing up, so that may have been a factor in the equation. It all worked out just fine, She knows this, and I love her dearly for the way it is. I count my blessings everyday.

What was interesting is that we had the name of the father, and even a postal address, I was eager to write a letter, especially having a great part of my life already in Hawaii. I was really curious.

I ended up writing to the name and address she gave me, but a few weeks later the letter was sent back, Return to Sender. I had no idea what would be the next step, besides, I was so exhausted mentally and emotionally. I really didn't want to do this part on my own.

At least now, Astrid and I were able to get to know one another more, and integrate this big change in our respective lives.

In 2005, I was still living in my unit, Astrid became a little more part of my everyday life, with a regular weekly visit, mail correspondence or talking on the phone.

I was spending more time with my parents. My Dad was in pain with ulcerated legs, getting them dressed every day with the blue nurses. He had a tough time with his body, he was very witty and sharp as a razor in the mind though. A little while back he was bitten by a white-tail spider. Flesh-eating necrosis was one of the symptoms. It was sad to see him in that way, very uncomfortable.

I know dad was getting ready to go. He was making sure Mum would be okay.

He started down sizing, selling off his factory units and doing business from his lounge chair. He was very efficient at getting things done and there was not one lazy bone in his body.

It wasn't the right time to pursue the other birthparent. I knew that, and it never feels right to go against what we know in our heart. It was just not the right time, period. I let it be for now and moved on with life.

CHAPTER 34

The birthday gift

A couple of weeks leading up to my birthday, I was busy massaging, paddling, and coaching the women. We had a strong team assembled and they were keeping me in good spirits. One of the girls on the team, Shandy, worked for a vet as an assistant and she mentioned this cat to me that was for sale. She kept saying how cute it was and that I would love it.

"What would I do with a cat?". I thought. "I like dogs."

Being in the unit, I never thought about pets. Anyhow, she planted a seed, and then a week later I went to the bank for my parents as well as the solicitors office, which happened to be next door to a vet clinic. It was the same company that my friend worked for but she was at a different location.

At the front of the clinic was a sign that said Kitten Adoption Centre.

"Hmmm," interesting I thought. My guidance told me to go in. It's like the invisible grabs your hand and leads you somewhere and you have no idea what's coming.

There in the front was an enclosure with the carpeted structures and squeaky play toys, I was being totally checked out by this cat. It was extremely alert and very forthcoming toward me.

I played with her for a little while and the girls were noting how she took to me. Of course they would, it would be lovely for all the kitties to have a home. I was captivated and in such joy playing with her. This feline definitely made an impact on me. I thought to myself, "Wow, could I really have a cat?" If I ever did, one like that one would be good. Her name was Lucinda. The girls kept encouraging me to buy her.

I left and thought about it for a little. I was going to Hamilton Island at the end of the week to race, so it was not good timing. However, I did think in the back of my mind, "If that cat is there when I get back, then maybe I get her. If it's meant to be, it will be."

Hamilton Island comes and goes. A week and a half later, It was my birthday.

Mum and Dad gave me this beautiful card. They wrote how wrote that they were proud of me and acknowledged me for what I do. They saw me. I didn't interpret this to be what I do on a physical level, but I got it at a much deeper soul level and it was really profound coming from my parents. As a spiritual being, on my path, I was being acknowledged. That was huge and very timely. I was taken back and very grateful. There was a hundred dollar bill in the card. I wondered how I would spend that, I wanted something really special and to be able to show them what the money went towards.

After talking story and gathering some things, I was off running some morning errands for them, I had to go to the bank for them and drop some papers at the solicitors.

I thought to myself, "Maybe I'll check to see if that little cat is still there, I may as well, I will be in the area."

After completing my tasks, I wandered over to the vet clinic. I didn't think she would still be there. She was too cute. Someone surely would have picked her up and taken her home by now.

I opened the glass door and went toward the enclosure and guess who came running over? I couldn't believe she was still there. This cat was gorgeous. How could anyone leave her there. Then I got the little flick in my neck, its like someone flicks you on the neck real quickly and it leaves a little sting, I call it a metaphysical clunk or a message from my spirit guides. They have different ways to communicate with us. One of the ways for me is that physical sensation on the side of my neck. I got my sign and my heart was so happy.

I took out my birthday money and paid for Lucinda, and I got a little adoption certificate. She had all her shots and was ready for a new home. I was so excited and it felt right. I knew Mum and Dad would be laughing about this.

I borrowed the cat cage, bought the kitty tray, all the stuff and the kitten Science Diet, she had to have best food! "Oh my god, I just bought a kitten."

I was so in awe. I couldn't believe it. She brought so much happiness into my life. We had a quick visit to my parents house to show them my new addition.

They were thrilled and loved her. Lucy was part of the family now. We had so much fun. She was like a dog more than a cat. We played and ran through my unit, she would skid across the bamboo floor chasing balls and toys. It was so lovely to come home to her at the end of each day.

She was such a blessing to me. The irony is that, Lucinda was the cat, that Shandy mentioned to me weeks beforehand. We put the information together and realized this was the same cat that was at her clinic. They had moved her down to the Burleigh Clinic to be adopted out. She was a divine gift to me without a doubt.

CHAPTER 35

Transition...

Late July Dad went into hospital with complications, the legs, the organs, everything was starting to give way. I know it was getting time. He was tired with the body. I was connecting with him strongly on a spiritual level. It was becoming easier for us to relate, the defenses were down, the human drama waning, and I knew his spirit was so strong and was getting ready to depart the body and this plane of reality.

I remember his last day. He was in hospital for a few weeks and I had been visiting him daily. This particular day, I went to school to teach, and fortunately I had kayak sports excellence and the kids were doing fitness. I ran with them around the nature preserve close to the school. I felt very serene in there and it was comforting to be in nature. I cried so many tears on the run, I didn't try hide to hide them, and the kids knew something was up. They were so amazing and completely on purpose in those moments. I finished my classes early and went straight up to the hospital. He was happy to see me, he couldn't talk much, but he was saying it all with his eyes, he was proud of me, understood me, and was satisfied with everything. It was time to go. Today was the day.

We had exchanged the look that is interpreted as "I know that you know, that I know, you know." I felt really happy for him because I knew he would be out of pain soon, they had him heavily dosed up on morphine so he was drifting in and out. He was ready. There was no fear present, just so much love.

I was saying my goodbye then, in private. It was just the two of us. My tears were minimal, I was reassuring him with my eyes and my energy that all would be fine. I am glad this happened. Our spirits calm and serene, I knew that was the last time I would see him in this form.

From the hospital I immediately went and bought myself a new pair of running shoes. Random, but I was following instinct. There was nothing to do, just being present and in the moment allowing inspired action. I ran the steps at Nobby Beach that afternoon for my dad. I dedicated that practice to him, as he was not able to use his legs for so long. It was my way of honoring him. I ran until I was physically exhausted and had nothing left. He passed later that evening peacefully with dignity.

I felt the exact moment he left the body, I was in my car driving and then I just started to wail. I have never made noise like that before. I could feel the release, the energies lifting, the clearing and then just normal tears. I was on my own in my car.

As I am writing this I know why. My family were all doing what they needed to do at that moment, what was best for us individually. There's more love in that freedom than I realized at the time. There was no expectation of what anyone needed to do, or where anyone needed to be. I love my family for this unconditional love. This greater love.

In the loving of you, you are loving of me.
In the taking care of Self at the deepest
level possible in any one moment
We are taking care of All.

I feel this in every cell of my being. Our needs vary through our individual experience and we must honor that.

I felt a place inside me where there was nothing. The void, a place that is free from judgement, and human influence, unaffected by anything we can see or even think. The absolute stillness and quiet so expansive. Maybe this is where God dwells, inside us. There was much comfort here.

CHAPTER 36

A Celebration of Life...

As with any loved one passing, there was the arrangements with the funeral directors, holding the service, and all the stuff that goes with it. We got through organizing all that, thank goodness. It was not easy, but everyone was so helpful. I was to speak at the service and do a eulogy. That was a piece of writing that was difficult to put together. I found it best to set intention and then trust that the words will come when they need to. Finally, the day before the funeral, the words came rushing through. I am so grateful for this process. It seems to be the way it works.

I was told that I need to have something written and in front of me just in case the emotion got too much. It surprisingly went without a hitch. Only at the very end in my closing remarks did it come rushing at me. I am so glad that I spoke that day. He heard me and was chuckling I am sure of it.

There is so much I could write here, be lead off into tangents, through family, different experiences, situations, relationships, but where this goes is not up to my logical mind. This story is about reunion, about spirit, about synchronicity and about me. The realization of the higher self and how that plays into our experience of life. We all have a story. How we view it, how we share it, and what we do with it, in the positive sense, is most important. If someone reads this and gets a lightbulb moment that awakens something within for their greater good and for the good of others, then there is purpose. If they get a laugh, or it reminds them or assists them in looking at something a little differently, then an objective is achieved.

CHAPTER 37

We Just Know....

A ugust 4, 2005 was the day my father passed. Life from this point was very different. We were all adjusting in our own way, getting through the formalities, as well as experiencing and releasing our personal grief from the physical loss. Dad, I am certain was "Happy as Larry" as they say in Australia. His spirit was free and soaring high with the birds. I seem to have an affinity with birds and the messages that I receive in their presence.

As a dear friend, Astrid was available to me and great support during this time. It was comforting to be able to chat with her.

A couple of days after the funeral, I went back to teaching, into a steady routine which was helpful. However, my heart wasn't there.

The truth was in my face, I really needed to make a move from school.

I was working my day to day routine, it was purposeful, and there was enjoyment. However, something wasn't feeling right. I know I just lost my father, but beyond that, it just didn't feel aligned. I was very raw, open and felt very connected with spirit, and it felt like I was being given a nudge into action. I am a teacher at the core of my being, however, it didn't fit. Something in me knew that my time was up. It's like our spirit, that inner voice turns the volume up so we can hear it's time to change something.

I was feeling so much guilt, how could I leave such a great job? Look at me. I work on the water, teaching kids, changing lives, receiving a good wage, benefits, all the bells and whistles yet still it was not enough to hold me down. I look back at the different experiences, the situations, all of it and maybe on the outside it looks like I couldn't commit to anything. Well, truth be told, I was committed to something much greater that was unfolding within me.

My spiritual path is my discovering of who I am not just biologically, with my ancestral roots, but of the Self, and of God, the true happiness, the true joy. Without that, there is an emptiness.

I didn't go to church or follow religious doctrine. I appreciate the practices, however I had done that many times before in past lives. I had been told this several times in readings.

We create our life, it is really our own dream, mixed up with others and it's interesting when I look back how complex I made it for myself to "know thy Self." That's the game we all play coming here, taking embodiment and experiencing life. Our higher self is directing the play, what happens is that we lose our Self in the game and we forget. The path then becomes one of remembrance and unfolding so that we can create from a higher perspective and connection.

Finding my roots was the logical thing for me to do. Ironically I have been taken in a direction that has given me far more than I would have ever imagined.

On my desk as I write at this moment, there is an inspiration card. In bold letters it reads,

"God's will is just beyond your plans."

I was having inklings of taking leave from teaching in 2006. I toiled with the idea. The normal worries about who will take over, who will do my job, how can they do it without me ran through the mind. I know for sure, that once we decide on something, the Universe (God) starts working it all out for us. We just have to take the first step, which is quite daunting initially, but once it happens, then we're in the flow.

A few months went by and the annual leave applications were due at school, oh the timing of everything! Here I was, filling in my form, that was a physical step of the process that had been decided months before.

I cannot tell you how much of a relief filling in the form was for me. I inhaled the deepest breath and exhaled with a sigh that was probably big enough to cause a strong breeze. It felt so good to be authentic and in my truth.

Everyone at school was so understanding and happy for me. It was time. From that moment on I really started to enjoy myself and make the most of my remaining days at school. The kids knew. They were very switched on, sad to see me go, but happy because they knew I would be in my joy.

I bless all those young beings I was so grateful to have with me during those times. They were totally on purpose, and the teachers I clicked with, what a gift. We had many a laugh. Some have since left and are following their dreams and passions which is great to hear. Maybe I helped to open the flow? We never know what one simple, truthful action may account for.

CHAPTER 38

Mana...

B efore school was out, there was another opportunity for me
to visit Hawaii, this time to paddle with Wailea, the Maui
club I paddled with some years back. Sarah's crew plus a few of
us from Australia and a couple from the US mainland.

I wasn't as fit as I had been in the past. However I was ready for
the race. It was my first time back in Hawaii after finding Astrid
and the information she had shared with me about my birthfather.

I met up with Maggie and Tim and we talked about our
common connection. I also felt extremely comfortable and even
more at home when I arrived Honolulu.

One of the girls from a Californian team was in the process
of finding her birthparents, so I could happily share a little of my
journey with her. We talked story over malasadas at the famous
Kanemitsu bakery on Molokai, the day before the race. There
were 3 of us at the table that were adopted, quite a sharing indeed.

This time we all stayed at the beach huts on Molokai Ranch,
beautiful, so very peaceful and serene. The pre-race preparation
very laid back and relaxing. Many a good conversation, plenty of
swimming and an easy and joyful time.

I couldn't believe I was back there on that special land. It had
been three years of so much going on, so much change, finding
Astrid, the passing of my father and all the experiences leading
into that.

When you race Molokai, and because it happens every year, the people are mostly the same to look at, but different inside. It's the one day where everyone comes together with the common bond of crossing the Ka'iwi Channel. Each year we return, there is change, loved ones lost, new life through birth, marriages, separations, beginnings, endings, so many stories.

All of the women gathered together, holding hands in prayer for the blessing before the race. There is this powerful "Mana" (energy) that comes over us all. Everyone has "goosebumps."

The chant in Hawaiian has every cell in my body and bones vibrating and ready.

It is a sacred ritual, a rite of passage, a blessing to all who paddle across the Ka'iwi channel. Just the blessing on race day was enough to have me come back for more each year.

On the way to Hale O Lono harbor I sat on the bus next to Michelle, my teammate from Kauai. All of a sudden I started to get hot. My palms so hot and the energy of the moment welled up inside, I mean there was a great deal of nervous energy in the bus.

Then a vision of my Dad, Big Bob, came in strong, I felt his essence, I felt him in that moment, and that this was a time of new beginnings for me. It was a good feeling, and Michelle knew what was happening. It was comforting to have her right there with me. The tears were streaming down my face. After a few deep breaths, the energy subsided and peaceful calm permeated my being.

About 6 hours later, exhausted and content the race was done. We stayed overnight at the Hilton Hawaiian Village, which is right at the finish line in Waikiki. It was my eleventh channel crossing. Our result placing was not up in the high rank as I had experienced previously, but it all was well. A great day spent with new and old friends, paddling across our beloved Ka'iwi Channel, I felt satisfied and full.

CHAPTER 39

Soul Food

I flew back to to the Gold Coast the night after the race, I had to finish off the school year.

Soon after my return, one of my long time paddling teammates, asked if I had a room to rent, she was forever having people stay and thought that maybe this might be a good connection, and some company for me. He was a gentle soul, not so much into partying, and he was needing a quieter space to stay in for a few months.

He was from Canada and was here racing and training for surf lifesaving. Swimming was one of his fortes and he was coaching at the local pool which was a stones throw from my unit.

It was a comfortable connection when we met, l was open to having company with me and it seemed to be a good fit. He was vegetarian, an athlete, someone who took good care of himself, and I appreciated this quality. During his stay, we traded skills, he taught me how to swim correctly and I was able to impart some kayaking technique to him. A quality exchange.

The one thing that left an impression on me was the way he cooked and prepared food. It was a complete mindful, conscious experience, so much care and love was infused into the food, and it was all vegetarian. This suited me fine, and it ended up being the inspiration for my food choices today. I didn't like to eat out after experiencing his cooking. I was in a new form of love. The nourishment, the nurturing through this food he was preparing was heaven for my soul. I could feel the vibration in the food and the way it was so carefully and lovingly prepared. It gave me a tangible awareness of how our energy effects everything, the way we go about our day, our thoughts we think, how we prepare our food, fold our clothes, and generally organize ourselves.

One particular evening I came home after a very stressful day teaching and the food was ready, on the table, pumpkin soup. I took the first mouthful, and tears came down my cheeks! I felt every morsel of flavor. God could not have shown up at a better time, it was a fulfilling experience. One mouthful of soup contained so much. It took me to a new level of appreciation. He was definitely an angel on my path. I was soo thankful.

Mindfulness in the small tasks can
have profound effects.
Life is a moving meditation.

CHAPTER 40

Christmas 2005

This was the first Christmas without Dad. I have never been big on Christmas. I appreciate the meaning and that is importance, but the rest of it, was never a big deal in our family. Maybe because my Dad didn't like Christmas, it brought up sadness and painful memories which equal stress. That alone explains why our family never went too far overboard with it. Each year it became less and less dramatic, more simple, and peace filled.

There was always the question of where to spend it, which relative was doing the dinner, whose bringing the turkey, what will we get so and so? Lets get to the stores before the rush etc etc...

For so many years I didn't even know, or even connect to the real meaning behind Christmas.

This time round, my sister had a newborn baby, Duke. He was just over a month old, I think her family may have been down south visiting her husband's parents. My Mum and I went to her brother's house. We were grateful for the invite, but really Mum wasn't in to it and I was quite neutral, just being there for her, and I think once we got home, we had quiet time together which was really enjoyable. The one thing I loved about my Mum, is that we could happily be in silence together, a really comforting and a still place for me.

The night before, I had spent Christmas Eve Danish style with Astrid. This was a complete contrast, very European, with some Danish delights. It was fun to experience some different foods. I know Astrid was so happy to spend this time with me, and it was the natural thing to do, our first Christmas together. At the time, my Mum and Astrid had not met. I had always hoped that they would become friends. They had a lot in common, me. One birthed me, one raised me and both loved me. They had also lost their partners recently.

We arranged for Astrid to come over to Mums place for morning tea early in the new year. It was wonderful for them to finally meet thankfully Astrid is a very good conversationist and my mum is great listener, the ultimate balance. Such a positive meeting for them both. I was so happy for this to happen.

Astrid travels a lot, quite a global child, and she would send Mum postcards from all over Europe, Denmark, London and places along the way. Every now and again she visits Mum and would her bring fruitcake or jam that she had made. It was mostly when I was there, but then I heard they were meeting without me around, which made me very happy indeed. At the time I was reluctant to share things too quickly. Some photos and things, baby photos no worries, but the early year pictures for some reason I wasn't so forthcoming. Who knows why. I honored how I felt and followed my intuition. Little snippets here and there, photos and then once mum warmed up, a few stories of my childhood and various memories would come forth. All was well.

CHAPTER 41

Be in the Na'au

I made a trip to Hawaii in February 2006. My friend Jimmy who we had met back in 2002 was getting married, this was happening on Molokai. It was an event, over 3 days. I was honored to receive the invite, and there were a couple of other Aussies friends attending and I just really wanted to get back to the islands even if for a little bit. You could say I was being drawn back in, and this was a great thing to be part of so why not? One of my teammates stayed in my unit and looked after Lucy the cat. My friends loved Lucy, because she was such great company to every one, a little ball of love! I was so excited to be going there, not to paddle races but to just be there and go with the flow.

I stayed with Paula and Chris. We had much to catch up on. Then the wedding weekend was upon us, such a wonderful celebration, I was amongst quite a few paddler friends on Molokai, but this time for good fun and celebrations, no pressure of racing, and it was a fabulous weekend.

I was so relaxed.

After the wedding I was keen to visit Maui to catch up with Sarah and take a trip to the Big Island now that I had more knowledge of my birthfather and where he was from. I was very, very curious to feel that place and do a little exploring. I so needed to do this. It was to be a journey on my own, with spirit guiding my way. I was really open and in that space of connection. It was to be a little pilgrimage of where I began. I felt like I was a sniffer dog looking for clues.

The first trip to Maui was courtesy of Jimmy, he was doing his hours for his pilot's license, I ended up flying with him in the back of a four seater plane, he and his instructor in the front and me and a big set of amplifiers in the back. They were transporting them to Maui for a party. It was ever so windy, and I was not laughing. Not even a squeak came from me the entire flight!

I was experiencing a little fear you might say. The boys in the front were laughing and telling jokes.

I was hanging on for dear life in the back. It was very bumpy, not fun at all for me. I remember Jimmy showing me the property on Molokai pointing things out, as we bumped along. Oh my god, I just wanted to get on the ground safely. Finally we touched down in Kahalui. I love that I was in good hands, and while they were laughing, I knew all would be okay. It was hilarious. Picture me in the back of a tiny plane with massive speakers and no where to go. Yes, the volume was starting to be turned up!

I spent the week on Maui and four of those days were in the training for my second Lomi Lomi course with my teacher. This was amazing, I was getting massage every day, and practicing.

We were doing stomach massage, working in the area of what the Hawaiians refer to as the Na'au - the gut, and they believe that on a larger scale the illnesses are often seen as emotional and/or spiritual in nature. Doubt, worry, putting other peoples truths before our own, all reveal a leaking of our spiritual power, our "Mana," our energy.

The Na'au is the total center of all experiential truths,
the path of power and knowingness they say.
Wisdom is in the Na'au, not the mind.

*Confusion and doubt are the result
of an argument between the mental mind and the Na'au.
The stomach is a real important area, we feel
it in the gut, and we have 'gut' instinct.*

The teachings were completely resonating with me, confirming so much of my experiences to date, the feelings, the intuitions and the following of my gut instincts. Hearing about the Na'au was great validation. For me to embark on this search for the pieces of my puzzle, I realized there was literally no other way I could do this. This was the path I was to walk.

The other thing that fascinated me was the Piko - or belly button. This is where the cording from others influences us, blood relatives through our umbilical cord, and then also psychic or energetic cords (aka) are held in that area. We learnt how to cut these cords (Oki) and release attachment. It all made complete sense. This belief system rang true with me. I completely understood, I took that out a little further into the Hawaiian culture and was having many insights into how some may have forgotten this knowledge, and how important it is if you are Hawaiian to know your roots.

I was digesting the information and integrating at the same time. It felt as if a big part of me knew this truth already. I was in the right place and the teachings seemed to be sparking something within.

My fellow students and I were learning many techniques and more of the Hawaiian philosophy behind the healing. I remember on the last day we did a meditation. It was focused on bringing the male and female aspect together as one, in ourselves and acknowledging our lineage on both sides, down the male side and down the female side. In the meditation, we really experienced seeing our mothers and fathers in a very high light. We were honoring the ancestral line, both the male and female, which is all part of us.

During the meditation I had another profound download.

This body is not only yours, it is of many.
It is our duty, our "kuleana" to take care of it.

It's like if someone gives you a car to drive for a period time, you are borrowing it, you don't own it, but you look after it as if it were your own, right?"

We honor our ancestors in doing this, and when we don't take care of ourselves we are in one way dishonoring them and ourselves. Not really knowing who my ancestors were, this journey made even more sense for me. It was important for me, somewhat on a personal level, but being the global child I am, it was much more on a cultural, collective level. Did I feel different after that week? Yes, very much so. There was a lightness of being, and I felt much more in tune and connected with source.

After a fun weekend with my friend Sarah, some laughter, paddling and great food at the local restaurants, I flew back to Oahu for a few days and then took my trip to the Big Island. I was ready for the next stage of the adventure!

CHAPTER 42

A Return to Source...

For this trip, my pilot friend Mike who I have mentioned earlier, gifted me a buddy pass to travel to the Big Island.

The week prior on Oahu, I did some searching for the birth father through the Tabernacle here in Honolulu. The Church of the Latter Day Saints have a big Genealogy Resource Center, and with the father's name that Astrid gave me, I became super sleuth and was researching on the computers for any clues. With the information I had, I was able to come up with a few names however none were remotely close, which was strange because there were quite a few names with that spelling.

I got tired of doing that because nothing was resonating. I wasn't getting any feeling so it was time to be open and be guided to where I needed to go, besides, that was part of the adventure.

I arrived in Kona, with no plans other than to get a car and drive. I did have some Australian friends who were living in Kona at the time so at some stage I was going to meet up with them.

In the meantime, the only car available was this huge four wheel drive. I felt like I was in a tank, but the good thing was, because I was on my own, driving all over the island with nothing but divine listening ears, it was probably a good thing. My intention was to see if I could feel my way to some clues, after all, the gut was heightened and very aware, I was open and unobstructed and ready for something! It was exciting for me. Maybe a little crazy, but who is to say.

I hung out in Kona and stayed overnight at the Sheraton Keahou Bay, which was close to my friends. When they finished paddling that evening, we had a barbeque. It was comforting to have a little structure to begin with, then in the safety of the hotel room, I scoured the phonebook, looking again for the birth fathers last name and seeing if I would feel or get any hunches of what to do next.

Nothing. So the next day. I decided to just get up and drive and acquaint myself with the Big Island of Hawaii. I drove out of Kona then over the Saddle Road and decided to go to where it all began. Back at Halemaumau crater, I paid homage to the volcano goddess, Pele, and then was drawn to the South Point area. From the information I received, my birthfather had spent a great deal of time there fishing and it was also the place where he had first met my birthmother and grandmother. Maybe my little spark of spirit came in when these two beings met.

It was a breathtaking drive to South Point, a road that runs all the way to the southern most tip of the USA. It was very remote, and you can imagine here I am, haole looking, blonde hair, lone female driving big ass four wheel drive down to the very southern most tip of the USA, all off the grid.

This is the kind of place you feel like you are in another dimension. Theres a definite power vortex here, I could feel it. I stopped and took pictures of these beautiful horses in the paddock, the land was lush and green and then there were all these broken, rusty, windmills. I guess a wind farm was the plan, they were not moving too much this particular day in February.

In this vast expansive area, eerily quiet but in a magical sort of way, I felt quite safe and comfortable. I pulled up at end where all the fishing platforms were, and I knew that this was the place where my birthfather would have been. Gosh maybe he was there that day fishing, There's a good chance, with what I know now.

At this particular time, I was none the wiser. It was important for me to just feel. I felt such a profound peacefulness, in a raw kind of way. The ocean was a multitude of blue, so very deep, possibly unforgiving, especially with the jagged lava rock cliffs it had carved out over time. The iwi birds flew overhead, and there were not many people in sight. I was truly out on the ledge there, a feeling of nothingness and so far away from what I knew my life to be.

There was a distinct energy I could feel and it was ancient and old. Even to be there, I felt like I had permission. Some places are not meant for visitors, and according to Hawaiian lore, they might say its forbidden or "kapu." I was tuning into this land and knowing I was connected in some way.

I drove some more and saw a sign for Green Sands Beach. This was where my birth mother and father met. I stood for a little while contemplating this and then decided it wasn't a good idea for me to go alone the 2-3mile walk in to the beach. I wasn't ready. At that point I remember not feeling safe and this was something that I wasn't going to experience on my own. There will be another time, I thought. I was just happy to be here, experiencing and marveling at the sight and feeling the remoteness of this landscape.

The next stop for me was Na'alehu, the town that was on the last address Astrid had given me. The address was no longer however, the town may give me some clues or at least a feeling.

It was quaint, and I really enjoyed it. I stopped by the local store, bought some food and was looking at the town around me. It felt very earthy and grounded to me. I liked it. I stayed for a little while, walked a little and then for some reason I found my self at the cemetery. I wasn't really thinking about anything, I just found myself parked by a tree and being still, listening for guidance and taking notice of the voice within.

He was not buried there, and he was still alive somewhere. That was my instinct. The logical mind was put to the side, and I just started to relax a little more and enjoyed the moment. "Look at where I am, in Hawaii, in the town that my birthfather is from." If that's as close as I get then, so be it. I am okay with that.

Acknowledging this, I decided it was time to think about getting to my lodgings for that night.

This is where it started to get amusing. I was headed back toward Pahoa, the Hilo side of the island. I had accommodation booked at Kalani Seaside Resort. By the time I got to the area it's dark, I am hungry, and I have little cell coverage. All I have is this big ass four wheel drive protecting me. I found myself in a strange neighborhood with no street lights. The stars were super bright, I was getting all dead ends, I had no idea where this place was.

I started to get a little nervous and didn't really want to drive back out to the main road. My mind was starting to play tricks and I was exhausted from a big day. Each time I tried to ring the resort to get directions, I couldn't get through and there was no one out on the streets to ask, if you have ever been around the Puna area, its sparsely populated and kind of jungle like.

I was getting really creeped out by this time. "What the hell am I doing out here all by myself, was I crazy?" I took myself purposely out on this limb, and all the fear was coming thick and fast. I was even crying. What's going on?

I'd had enough. I stopped the car and got out. Middle of nowhere, dark as all dark, yet the stars were so bright, I looked up and prayed for help. Please god help me find this place. Some deep breaths later, I was then in a state of awe and wonderment with where I was, my fear had left. I got back into the car and drove a few minutes just going with the flow and the next thing you know I see the sign for the resort! I was so happy and relieved. Mahalo Ke Akua, Thank you God.

The next morning I walked down to the beach. It was beautiful, very raw, rocky, not swimmable in that particular area, but I saw turtles and had some quiet time in meditation.

On the way out from Kalani later that morning, I found the steam vent just off the highway that I was told about. I was wearing way too many clothes, but I walked a little way in the forest and there it was, the steam coming up. Madame Pele welcoming me into a nurturing space.

I found my way into this little cave, there was a seat made out of blocks and a wood plank and I sat and felt the soft steam, the warmth of the island. I felt like I was inside nature's womb. It was so comforting, a little smelly with the sulfur, so I didn't stay in too long. In Hawaii, you can be nurtured by being with the elements, the warm ocean ponds, sitting by a steam vent, exfoliating with black sand at the beach and having a spa under a waterfall, now that's my kind of pampering! Mother Nature, always providing and nourishing us.

CHAPTER 43

'HA'

My whirlwind trip to Hawaii was full of adventure. This time it was not about paddling with teams or doing races, but paddling my own event, my personal life experience and all of its unique paths, reconnecting with friends, quality ocean time, celebrations and discoveries. I experienced three islands in a little over two weeks and accomplished much.

When I finally flew out from Honolulu on route to Australia, I had such a well of emotion build and so many tears as the plane departed and left Waikiki in the background. The energy moving through me was intense. There was much emotion and the person beside me was probably thinking I was crazy. If we have to emote, we have to. It's energy moving through us. We cannot hold it in. I heard the rains came the next day, and did not stop for forty days. I missed that thankfully.

Back on the Gold Coast I was officially on leave from school, massaging clients from home and coaching the Surfers Outrigger girls. A group was forming to go to the World Sprints on the North Island of New Zealand in March. My sister really wanted to go and use it as motivation to get back into shape after having baby. She has Maori roots, so it was a good place for her to go paddle and connect with the land. She didn't do a search for her biological parents, but nevertheless had a strong spiritual pull towards that culture.

The group of girls I was coaching and paddling with were from different backgrounds. Energetically, the dynamics of bringing this team together was probably one of the most challenging for me. There were a couple of newbies to Outrigger coming from other paddle sports, some experienced girls and then my sister and me. This particular gathering of souls was an interesting one, very diverse personalities. The intention here was acceptance.

In the canoe, everything must all be put to the side.
You bring your best self.
You become one with the canoe and leave
the human drama behind for a while.
This is the only way the boat will
move forward with ease.
We are all the spokes in the one wheel.
Everyone plays a part and all are
important.

We were not world beaters but there was reason for us all gathering in the way we did. Don't know exactly what the reason was but, no coincidences, we trained hard, did as much as we could in four months and enjoyed the experience. It was certainly fun visiting New Zealand, I also got to see my paddling friends from Hawaii.

What was quite interesting for me when I was there, was one day in particular. All the Australians were as a group together in uniform, all the Hawaiian team were close by easily identifiable and I can tell you in that moment I felt I was more part of the Hawaiian team than the Australian team.

Strange you might say, yet it just felt natural. I had some down time contemplating there at the lake, watching races, staying neutral, and I remembered one afternoon, we had presentations.

It was a beautiful sunset over the lake, and then clear as day, the message was downloaded. It was time for me to move to Hawaii.

I decided there and then in the neutral place, the islands between Australia and Hawaii, part of the Pacific triad, I call it. New Zealand was like the child, Australia and Hawaii the parents, and I was on middle ground, or middle earth you might say!

It was done. Everything started to shift. Once a decision is made that is in alignment, the pieces start shuffling, the thoughts, the vibrations go out like ripples on a pond. I tossed the pebble into the lake that day.

Once the racing was done, one of my team mates and I rented a car and took a short trip north to check out the country. It was during this time that my creative spirit came alive. I have was so inspired by watching Lynwen taking closeups of plants with the camera. I found myself following suit. I was getting up close and personal with the flowers!

It was so much fun. I found myself even using the breath by breathing quite purposely into each shot. I didn't intend it mentally but "something" was breathing me. Later I find out that the "HA" in Hawaiian is known as "the breath of life." The HA breath was coming through me. That something is spirit, God, what ever you wish to acknowledge that unseen force. I felt such a lightness of heart whilst taking the photos. I was in pure joy.

It was the start of a photo collection which I entitled Haumea Creations in honor of the Hawaiian Earth Mother Goddess "Haumea." It seemed very appropriate considering where I was on my journey. For me I really feel she is the Mother of all Mothers. New Zealand was the spark needed to light things up, move things forward for me. The photography, and of course the decision to move to Hawaii. I didn't know how on earth that was going to happen, but I knew deep down it would all work out just fine.

I arrived back on the Gold Coast in March 2006. We had a short break from paddling, so I went to Sydney for three weeks, I was just needing a change, and integration space. This was transition time. A big life decision always affects those around you in some way, so an adjustment time is helpful. So much had happened in the last couple of years. I was giving myself a moment to catch my breath. Spending time in Manly was fabulous for me, again just a whole different environment, I wanted a break from the outriggers too, and had to decide what the next step was in that area. I decided while I was away that I would finish off the season.

When I returned I was training for the Hamilton Cup, my last one for the club. After many years, the club was changing names and venue so it was rather fitting. I really wanted to make this one special and assembling a team that could do the job was my intention.

As paddler coach of this group, I went about writing a plan, also a vision of how I would see it coming together, this was another inspired writing coming through me. We were to have a meeting one night with all the girls and just put out what was needed and required. I had only just finished writing it about half hour before we were to meet. I printed the sheets to hand out. This was going to be a little bit different from what had happened in the past.

We always had vigorous time trials and hearts were broken and paddlers lost along the way. This time we set the intention for the boat to show truth. The idea of having a higher power be in

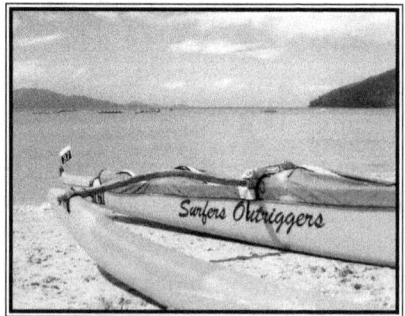

charge was introduced and a couple of us would facilitate the physical practices.

I thought to myself, this is who I am and I cannot do it any other way than to speak truth and even try this. I was ever so grateful for the group of open minded talented women that were available at the time. We had twelve girls, and interestingly enough, due to work commitments and injury, two girls could not attend, and right there we had our team!

The girls that dropped out were just as good paddlers, but for this particular experience, the team naturally formed. We did a fabulous job coming together, second in the big money race and places in the sprints and round the island race. I was satisfied with that, The girls were happy, the club was happy. It was my last hurrah there, I knew I would be in Hawaii next time around.

It felt complete. Surfers Paradise Outriggers went full circle, right up to where it was getting ready to be a new club, and since I left, the club went from strength to strength, winning the Hamilton Cup Change race for the first time recently and many other races. You always know when its time to step aside, If you are quiet and listen, the guidance always comes through.

Hard to believe my whole existence revolved around this paddling. It has been the common thread, the glue that has kept me in a protective and safe circle, yet has allowed the expansion of who I am both biologically and spiritually. I am in awe.

Do you ever start doing things unconsciously, you don't plan to do them, but it just happens, there's no set date, or actual event down in the diary, but you have a feeling, and then you start going into action spontaneously. After Hamilton Cup, I started downsizing, throwing old clothes out, organizing papers, all sorts of admin stuff, general culling of material possessions, I was giving away clothes, books, all sorts of items. Boxing things up, clearing space and putting things in order. I was still massaging my regular clients, hanging out with Astrid a little and spending time with my family.

CHAPTER 44

Trust your path...

One afternoon in July, I got a phone call from an organization promoting a big seminar in Sydney for early September, the title of the seminar was called "Unleash the Power Within" by Anthony Robbins. I wasn't one for getting the over the phone sales push, however, I did find myself giving the guy on the end of the line, a little more time than usual.

I had a couple of his books and had listened to a CD, but had no intention of ever seeing him live in person. Since my human potential seminar days, I really had not done anything like that for a long time. My interest in transformation was always ripe, understandably and I was walking a spiritual path, something was feeling good about this. I didn't make an instant decision but I know the order of things is always pertinent, and I told the guy to call in a week and I would see we're I was at.

I knew I was going to be doing it as he hung up. I gave myself the cooling off period and a week later signed myself up. It was the impetus I needed to take my next step which was moving to Hawaii. Now I could work on dates to depart from Sydney and I would coincide it with the seminar. Perfect.

I have a few friends in Sydney that I have stayed with over the years. So gracious with their hospitality, whether it was a longer stay in Manly with Shelley and Guy, a quick pick up and roast meal with Kristy and James or an inner city apartment, complete with a cat, Thanks to Aaron. This time it would be different, I wasn't feeling to stay with anyone, I was happy to book in a nearby city hotel, within walking distance so that I could come back each day and integrate quietly with Self. Yes, that was the way for this time.

Still there was some things to do. I set the date for my departure to Honolulu. I didn't have a job. I didn't know how it was going to happen, but I knew it would all work out fine.

I was going to go for three months, which was the visa time limit, and during that time I would check things out.

There was excitement, and hesitation, but I knew this was the right thing to do, my life was already in Hawaii. I knew deep inside, that I was to be there and where things would open up for me. The calling was loud, and there was no other way to go. My whole adventure to date has been one of listening, opening up, releasing old emotional baggage, emptying out enough to be able to bring in light and more love for Self and therefore others. Following our bliss, and joy, no matter how simple is key. It leads us to our unique and profound path.

I wanted to come home, the home in the sense of spirit. You can be home where ever you are, but the home inside with the Self is the one where you are never lost, or found. You are your light and you are a beacon for others. It's not an easy path. Its work, releasing and surrendering to something much larger. Taking the mind out of the way, and piercing the veil of illusion we have ultimately created for ourselves. Endeavoring to understand our own game. Our unique play of consciousness. It is in our best interest to enjoy the ride.

When God speaks and you are in a place
to truly listen, with your heart,
body, mind and soul all things point
in that divine direction.
It may seem difficult for the people you leave behind,
but truly, on this path there is no other way.
Following your own truth, listening to your heart
is your dharma (duty) and in doing your own
dharma even if its not perfect, it is better than doing
another persons dharma exceptionally well.

CHAPTER 45

What about Lucy?

At the time I was practicing yoga at a studio in Broadbeach. After class one morning I was having coffee with some fellow students. They all knew I was getting ready to leave for Hawaii, and someone asked me about Lucy my cat.

I still didn't know what to do there, I would have gladly taken her, however, I didn't even know where I was going, plus with quarantine, the plane ride, it seemed a little hardcore for a cat.

The fact was, that I decided I would have to give her to someone. That tore me up a little.

I wondered who that person would be. This cat had been such a great companion it was going to be hard to leave her.

One of girls said that a girl from our class was looking for a cat. I was keen to find out more, so I ended up meeting her and then she came to visit Lucy at my unit. Lucy took to her nicely and I decided that this was the person that would love and take care of her. I was relieved. Sad, but relieved.

The night before I was to take her to her new home, we had an experience. I had her on my lap and patting her, and then I turned her over and she was laying on her on her back, she fully stretched out and opened heart to me. That's what I thought at the time. It was a complete surrender. She had never relaxed on her back before, so this was a different mode for Lucy.

A special moment for us both. I love animals for their purity of being and unconditional love, so blessed we are to have our furry friends.

I felt that she knew this was our goodbye, but it was also, an acknowledgement that she would be on purpose, giving much needed love to the next girl, and she was letting me know that she was ready for her divine assignment. I wondered if I was ready.

The next day was tough. We had a proper goodbye the night before, now the formalities. I had to go to the vets to borrow a cage to transport her in. On the drive there, I just started bawling. Here we go. It was so deep. My birthmother shot into my awareness. There was a huge understanding for her right in that moment. I am just giving a cat away! Brilliant how the universe brings us insight and awareness. The triggers we experience, seemingly innocent and unrelated.

Finally I dropped Lucy at her new home. It was a little strange, but she had all her toys, the food, the litter tray, everything, and I had to leave her there, she was going to be fine. Me, well, I knew that this was the way, it sucked at the time but it was the only way, and Lucy knew. I said my aloha, and got in the car quickly. Like clockwork, driving home, the heavens opened up, the rain poured down, a releasing, a rainbow, blessings from above. Keep going... **Breathe**

CHAPTER 46

Preparing for Take off

The next day I watched from my kitchen window the removers truck now fully loaded with all my furniture packed high, drive away. That was my life of the last few years. My couch that so many had sat on, drank tea upon, slept on. My fridge, my bed, book shelf, table chairs, all of it, I let it go, it all went in one swoop. No mucking around now. It felt liberating. Now we are getting down to the wire. The unit needed to be cleaned. Astrid helped me do this. We had a fun time getting it ready. I put it up for rental with an agent and then I spent the last few days on the Gold Coast with my mum.

Journal Entry August 31, 2006
The week had come and gone. I got through it. What an emotional roller coaster. A limbo period. Uprooting my home, my sanctuary.
I am happy my sister organized a couple of friends to come over for a farewell dinner. I am now looking forward to starting a fresh in Hawaii. I can't wait. Not long now.

Journal Entry September 2, 2006
"I am listening to a melody of car horns hearing it as a celebration of life? Interesting perspective... I am really enjoying the Anthony Robbins

experience. I walked on fire last night, that was amazing." Cool moss, cool moss, cool moss...
I met some great people and had a high five from the big man himself, he has the hugest hands by the way. Tomorrow will be great, He is validating me and my experiences, it's another piece in the jigsaw puzzle and I feel right on track. So glad I decide to come."

That weekend went by quickly, it was so good to know that I was on route to the rest of my life.

I literally packed up what I knew, had one suitcase in the hotel room, and I was completely in present time. Surrounded by great inspiration, much creative energy and plenty of momentum, it was totally happening. What was amusing is that Tony would often during the weekend mention, "How much do really want something and what are you willing to do to make it happen?"

I was doing it. I knew that I was living on the edge of my life and stepping into the unknown.

He would so often describe the feeling. I just kept giggling to myself, that's me he's talking about, I am doing it. It was good reflection for me. I was in alignment. It was more confirmation and validation of what I already knew and what I was currently experiencing in my reality. I was really going for it.

Journal Entry September 5, 2006

"Oh my goodness, I am finally sitting on the QF3 bound for Honolulu! I am excited in every cell of my body and at the same time looking forward to sleep.
Today was an absolute breeze. Spent lunchtime with an old teaching colleague at the Cruising Yacht Club of Australia. What a beautiful last day in Australia for me, absolutely divine. I am feeling so blessed."

I slept well enough on the plane and after breakfast, I find myself journalling again.

"We are on the descent now. Oh my god, I cannot believe I am here. I am going to be stepping foot on Hawaiian soil very soon. Theres a baby screaming but I don't care. I am so excited."

CHAPTER 48

My other Home, Hawaii....

It's all go from here. I put a lot on the agenda for my arrival. Sarah picked me up, with Duke the dog and we had lunch at Bogarts. I got my phone charged up, and then was getting dropped up the road to meet Gena, who I had planned to go to the Big Island with. She had organized three days at a retreat, and I felt it would be the best way for me to groove into life here, ground down and be in nature. That night we had to be at the airport for a 7:45 flight and we hit the largest traffic jam Oahu has ever experienced. The headlines the next day read "STUCK"

We ended up missing the flight and consequently, even the last flight of the night. It took two and half hours to travel 5 miles. Crazy. If it wasn't for our luggage we would have walked. Rather than have the people drop us again in the morning we decided to stay in the airport hotel, save the trouble and get out early the next day. We had Jamba Juice and Cheetos for dinner because nothing else was open. We finally arrived in Kona the next morning and after a quick breakfast with another friend, we drove to the other side of the island.

Sapphire, lived in a beautiful house in a gated community just outside of Pahoa, with her own warm thermal sea pond that fluctuates with the tides, she even had in her care a 35 year old sea turtle named Honu.

The property was so tranquil and relaxing it was beyond time and this world. She was a spiritual teacher and just like a fairy godmother you could say. The two of us were learning and connecting deeply with nature. We went and left an offering for Pele at the Volcano and while we were there I ran through this side track barefoot for about 5 mins full blast. I had so much energy. It was pure joy. I looked forward to working my body, it's been so long since I have wanted to do anything.

When you are working mentally and shifting energy and making changes, it's quite exhausting! We played nature nymphs for a few days, totally being nurtured by the island. What a blessing to be there and in high spirit company. It was the perfect opportunity to allow my gifts to surface some more.

September was a month of settling in. In Honolulu I was massaging paddlers who were getting ready to race the channel. I decided that for this years race, I would be on the shore at the finish line this time. I was happy to finally march to the beat of my own drum. It was an honor to be asked by different crews to race with them, but essentially, at this moment I was wanting to paddle my own canoe so to speak. I was already midchannel of my own race!

One very cool experience in the following week, was a day out on Kanehoe Bay, with Donna from Kai Makana. She had a group of New Zealand school students visiting and thought I might enjoy hanging out and helping them with the paddling and canoe sailing. They performed a Haka for us. It was very special and extremely moving, life was showing me so much magic.

Journal Entry September 17, 2006

"It was interesting to spend time with Donna, this girl has paddled on a one man canoe across all the channels in Hawaii, island to island in effort to bring more awareness to the ocean and its life. We were talking about the water and I had no idea, that the PH level of the human body (7) is the same as the ocean. The other thing we talked about, was the fear that comes up with the ocean. For a long time I was relating to it as something apart from me, and not of me. Yet I am one with it. I think that is what I was experiencing earlier this year.

There have been certain bodies of water that I have not felt the mana or much energy coming from it. At particular times especially on the canals where I used to train, I literally have felt my energy, drain out of my arms and not because I was paddling hard. She was saying that certain water can drain you because there is no life force in it and it is a conductor of energy. I know there are books written on this. Maybe the more open I was becoming, the more sensitive I was to the different kinds of water and my awareness was heightened. Sometimes I could not understand why I didn't want to paddle.

CHAPTER 49

Show me the way

There is much happiness in my being and every day is the blessing. I would wake up to the sound of the turtle doves and I couldn't help but smile. I was staying with Paula and Chris in Manoa, so I walked everywhere, we would often meet for coffee at the marketplace, and different people would show up to talk story and share on those mornings.

Journal entry - September 19, 2006
Download for the day...
"I am wanting You to have fun and enjoy every minute of your day. Open hearted, connect with people, animals and mother nature. Be relaxed and confident in yourself allow your inner and outer beauty to radiate today. You deserve it."

When I write in my journal, there are moments where I am getting a directive from spirit, so if there is a message, or download I write it and then follow. During this time I was writing a lot.

With that message in mind, I walked down to Manoa marketplace and had coffee with Jimmy and Chris. Jimmy practices in the healing arts and is very in tune, it was refreshing to connect with him and talk shop. Later that day I caught the bus with Pamela, Mikes cousin to Sea Life Park. It was so fun to see the animals. We met her Japanese friend who works there as a trainer and she took us back to the turtle nursery. I got to hold a baby turtle. They are so cute, and there were dozens of them, I also saw an array of interesting creatures including a unicorn fish, I liked him!

There was also a Hawaiian monk seal and a Wolphin! (A mix of whale and dolphin)

When the dolphins came out to do their thing, I had a well of energy (emotion) come out. I definitely have a strong connection with these delightful beings, It's the best mirror reflection for myself the happiness is overwhelming when I am in their company!

Journal Entry September 26, 2006

Okay, Living in Hawaii? Can U please clear a path as to where you would like me to live? Make it known when the time is right. I wish this process to be easy and flowing without confusion or hassle. When you feel it is ready please bring it into my awareness in a harmonious way....
Thank you. "How do I get to stay in Hawaii? What is my next course of action? I am looking for insight"

Journal Entry September 29, 2006

"What an interesting few days I have had. I feel the dust has settled. Felt forced into something that didn't feel quite right, it seemed perfect for me however very happy with my decision. I felt some pressure this week and I held my own, I am very proud of myself, keep breathing deep, it will all work out just fine.

The journal continues to be my way to connect with spirit, and communicate through my questions and writing.

When things get a bit muddled, and if state of confusion hits, time to take a trip to an outer island. In particular for me, it is

Kauai. I went with Shelley and Guy who were visiting with their family. It was just what I was needing.

We dined in Hanalei and my friend Gabriela and her canoe teammates just finished hiking the Napali Coast and this was there first proper meal in a few days. They were excited. I'm continually blown away at what a small world this is. You never know who you will meet when you are in the flow. It is always magical when you are truly following and moving with spirit.

Kauai is so beautiful. I feel very clear and experience much clarity each time I visit there. I liken that island to the crown chakra, which is our link to the universal source of energy.

Always on Kauai, I get the greatest insight and my intuition is at its peak. I love that island. It's an older island, very wise and so expansive, and so green and lush. It's my heaven.

As I recall these times, there is a little island hopping going on, I have put intention out there, now I am just having a little fun while the next thing unfolds, not waiting, It's already happening, everything unfolding as it should.

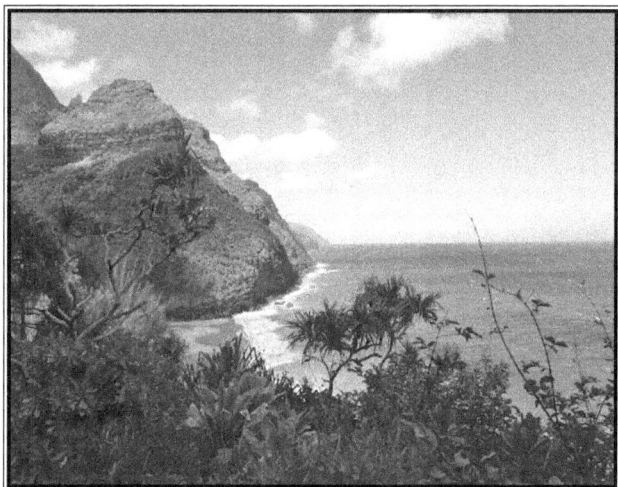

CHAPTER 50

Time for a Shake Up?

Mid October I was on the Big Island. We all went for Walter's birthday party in up country Waimea. That was a real treat we stayed on his parents ranch, and had a variety of activities before the actual party night, horse riding, motorbikes, hiking, to name a few. I remember taking a walk with Gaby and Jacki we saw a rooster high up a tree I thought at the time, it was a little strange.

Before arriving that day, I took a drive on the Saddle Road and drove up Mauna Kea. I talked story with a guide there, who was well travelled and knowledgeable. This was somewhere I wasn't really familiar with. I had read about the goddess Poliahu, the bringer of order without force, she has the gentle caress and nurturing nature. I couldn't help but think about her. We always hear so much about Pele, the fire and the upheaval, I felt I was paying homage to her cooler counterpart. I love all this stuff. It i interesting and wonderful to know the mythology behind the various gods. Its a big part of Hawaii, and the culture, so I take the time to learn and listen.

The party that night was fun. I had many of my friends there and felt right at home. I am not a big drinker and although there was an abundance of everything, I was fairly easy on the wine and food and went to bed around 11pm. I got up in the middle of the night, went to the bathroom which was outside. I looked up and the stars were so bright, you could see them all. I had the strangest thought going through my head at the time.

"I wonder what my ancestors sound like?" Now that's kind of random, maybe it was the wrong question to ask, forgive me if it had anything to do with the next morning at 7.15am!

We woke to the shuddering vibrations of the earth, the pictures on the walls were falling and glass was shattering, It was a 6.5 Earth quake moving like a freight train through the property. The people outside who were cleaning up literally saw the ground fold and move, I was reading. My friend in the other bed beside me was still sleeping, when we were jolted quickly out of comfort zone.

She didn't have her contacts in and was super scared, so she grabbed me and then we got outside the room to a safe space, everyone was fine. A little shaken but not stirred. That was so much energy, and it scared the living daylights out of me. I was grateful to be there and not somewhere else, I had friends, I was safe and we had supplies and food. I wasn't going anywhere in a hurry. We were away from the pandemonium and that was a godsend.

I wrote in my journal later that morning......

"I am feeling so wiped out right now. I am scattered and just wanting to relax myself by sitting in this hammock.

There are aftershocks. I have my feet up against a tree and I am breathing much better now." She has shaken the fear out now, who would have picked today."

My immediate reaction once I got out side was to put my hands on the earth which I did to calm "her" down, to calm myself down. I really felt into that and was tuning in, even though there was much going on, I tried my best to stay present. I felt all this sadness and just wanted to cry. I really needed calming down now. The dogs from the neighbors farms all came running into the ranch, 3 of them came straight to me, it was so comforting and I was happy for this. It was just the tonic!

My adrenalin was pumping very fast. Jimmy was laughing at me, I had my small backpack and was folding my clothes, it was all I could to do to feel some sort of order in the external chaos.

I guess that was my response at the time. Some people continued to clean, I needed to be alone and in my own space just for a little while, it was a lot to process. There was much energy in my system. Most people at the party have experienced one before, I had not. It was my first time.

I thought to myself what the hell am I doing moving here to Hawaii. I just wanted to go home. Mother earth released a great deal of energy that day!

CHAPTER 51

New Connections

From what we heard it was a little messy out and about on the roads. Rocks and trees had fallen, and it felt safer to stay put rather than go anywhere. I was in the best place I could possibly be in at the time, and in no hurry to leave. Thoughts of pitching a tent right out in the middle of the paddock appealed to me, no trees, nothing to fall, just wide open space to feel the aftershocks and be safe and away from the action would have been fun. The horses on the property were a bit skittish from the tremors, so I spent much of my time around them during that day. The animals sense things very well maybe the chicken up the tree the day before was a sign?

The next day when things had settled some more, it was time to drive back into Kona, I was to drop the car at the airport and would be picked up by Kenny and his Kiwi friend Paul, who I met for the first time. He was a kindred spirit. We connected instantly and spoke the same language you might say. He was very open spiritually and was wanting to feel and experience certain areas of the Big Island. We figured it would be fun to play tourist and visit the spots together that interested us. The next day, we would hire a car and go explore.

Kenny's partner Lucy met up with us that morning, and we took a drive to the end of the road, checking out the damage from the earthquake. We hiked into Pololu Valley. Absolutely beautiful. Black sand beach, lush forest and very peaceful. That night, I was so wired, I couldn't sleep at all, so much happening, so much energy!

The next morning I practiced yoga with Paul on the deck, and after a quick ocean swim in Kona, we prepared for our adventure.

Journal Entry October 17, 2006

"We are going to have the most magical day, we are hiring a car and going south. Today is the day to focus on the positives and what we are wanting respectively in our lives and this will be accelerated by being together with positive intention.
I feel so blessed and thankful for my life" Namaste......"

Lucy and Kenny dropped us off at the airport to get a car. Paul was really wanting to visit the Volcano and I wanted to visit Green Sands Beach, where my birth father and mother had met. Last time I was on my own. This time I had a friend to accompany me. We ended up getting there in the heat of the day, and the walk down was so hot, I felt bad that I had roped him into doing this with me, but he was such a good sport, carrying the bag, the water, the camera and we looked a treat, as if we were walking across a desert into the unknown, seeking the oasis. I kept thinking, it's just over this next rise but it wasn't quite like that. It took a little while longer than I originally thought. We finally could see the bay open up, Green Sands Beach. Oh my god, it was beautiful and rather mystical being there.

The sand was glistening green with thousands and thousands of Olivine sparkles and the occasional larger piece. (Olivine is the crystal known as Peridot) and this beach is full of it.

For those that know me, know that I love my stones and the meanings behind them.

Peridot is said to be a stone of prosperity, and on an emotional level helps to remove blockages to receiving, among other things.

As we made our way down the slope to the beach, I was feeling so much joy, and I was letting it all flood in. I felt so free and light. It was as if my spirit knew it was home, playing and frolicking and just being so happy.

A wave of beauty, magic and mystical energy came upon me. I had so many insights flow through me. I think back to that time and that feeling, that was me, at my essence, that was where I came into being. If we could have a place where our spirit or soul enters the earth plane, if it is in fact a physical place, then this is where I came to be, this was my entry point, right here. My spirit birthplace so to speak!

Paul was very mindful and knew the significance of this trip for me. He sat back on the sand and just observed and watched me frolic and come to life. He took a few random pictures of me playing and wow, I felt so happy at the core of my being. This is how I intend to be. This is me right here, light hearted, playful. It was so refreshing.

I was honoring my beginnings. Back to the source and having a playmate to share it with on that day. I am sure he was a playmate of mine somewhere through times passed. Felt so blessed to have the company and to be able to share the experience. After swimming and playing we trekked back to the car.

We were hot and sweaty yet happy and very content. Next stop was Volcano National Park, time to visit Pele.

By the time we got to the park it was nearly closing, but we went in anyway. It was so still, not many people at all, and it felt very auspicious being there. My friend was very sensitive to the energy here and it was his turn to revel in the light. This time I was the observer and happy to be there supporting his experience.

It is so incredible the way the universe places the people on your path, at various stages of your journey. It is always so perfect. I felt like I was so full of light and love, full blown earth mother / goddess energy, unconditional, loving and open. I was meant to be there to hold that space and be reflection for him to feel his light, his spirit and strength.

The higher or spiritual significance of people coming together becomes apparent, sometimes sooner than later. If it is just for a fleeting moment, or for many shared moments, grace is bestowed upon us and the blessings are infinite. It is an advantage to be awake and to be conscious enough to receive the insight.

What a magical day. I have my kiwi brotherly love, and my spirit came home to feel joy again in this beautiful land that is still growing and rumbling, connecting us with the deepest parts of our soul.

*I feel that when we visit certain places that are calling
us, we collect the pieces of ourselves we left behind
along the way. It's fascinating when we get see, feel and
experience different places, people and different energy.
There is remembrance on many levels
that we are not even conscious of.
We essentially feel our way home.*

November 6, 2006 Journal Entry

*Ten weeks in Hawaii. I have somewhere to live, somewhere beautiful by
the way, I have a job to come back to. I am so grateful. Mahalo Ke Akua
for making it possible and for the continuous free flowing creations. I
am so excited about what has occurred to date. I am truly honored. I am
deserving of only the best. I am so grateful for such wonderful friends,
they are all helping in my life and we are sharing experiences together. I
am proud of myself for going ahead with it all. It feels wonderful to ac-
complish this goal. I am excited about my life."*

During this time of creating I was journalling and writing
a lot. This was important, in the creation process because I am
communing with God and Self, with honesty and without judgement. I am writing intentions like they are going out of fashion,
and I cannot believe how many words I have handwritten, but I
know they were absolutely necessary.

CHAPTER 52

Dot the I's and cross the T's... Australia

I had some things to do, preparations for visa requirements. I had a job.

Before all that starts it was time for a little celebration. I had a couple of nights in Sydney and went to the U2 concert at Stadium Australia with my friend Aaron. He had never been to a concert of that calibre, it was definitely going to rock his socks off. U2 is my favorite band. I have listened to that music for a long time, they are timeless. Bono the lead singer is inspiring with his message, his platform through the music, expressive, bold, outgoing, gifted and influential, completely on purpose.

It was an electrifying experience with 100,000 people in attendance. That's some energy field.

Bono and the boys casually walked out under the light to the stage. They took their time, with nothing to prove for them, contributing to this planet through their music and their message.

This makes me wonder how I wish to contribute.

On the subject of contribution, I now have the opportunity to serve the kids of Hawaii. It's exciting. I was offered the position of Head Coach/Program Director of Hawaii Canoe and Kayak Team - a non-profit organization formed in 1988 as a way of developing the paddling talent in Hawaii and provide a pathway which could take them all the way to the Olympics. It was an honor and a privilege as those that had been involved and who had set up program many years prior are all well known and respected watermen, very accomplished in the paddling community, good people giving back. It was a perfect fit for me, to be here in Hawaii with an opportunity for me to give back to the place and the people that have given me so much.

After some visa formalities in Sydney at the American consulate, I was to be back in the islands and to start work straight away. It all happened very quickly, much support and hospitality, great kids to coach, and supportive parents, a perfect transition to living here. My routine swiftly began each day with a 5am alarm and by 5.30am the kids and I would be in our kayaks paddling into the sunrise on the Ala Wai Canal.

As for searching for the birthfather, I had hit a dead end, so I let go for a moment and continued with life making the most of everyday and contributing in the best way I could. I was living with a wonderful family in Kahala, in a studio at the back of their house. My place was walking distance to the ocean and very convenient to a shopping centre and bus line. The roads were bike friendly in that area. Initially without a car, I walked, rode bike, and took the bus. I was blessed with the occasional ride from friends as well. All flowed well.

The kids I coached were awesome. After a few months training, I took a small group of athletes to the National trials at the Olympic Training Center in Chula Vista, San Diego. In summer we were in Lake Placid New York for the National Junior Development Camp for which I was one of the coaches and then in August each year is the US National Championships. We visited Seattle, Oklahoma City and Lake Lanier in Georgia. The

Hawaii kids loved to travel and were great ambassadors for the state, spreading the aloha wherever they went.

CHAPTER 53

Surprise news.....

In 2007 I was keen to paddle outrigger and was honored to receive a few offers and decided to paddle under Coach Raven at Hui Lanikila. I had friends in the crew and it was refreshing to arrive at practice and not have to set a session or run one. I could just pick up the paddle and go.

Such a delight and I really appreciated that time. When we teach, or coach, it is important to take the time out for ourselves and remember to do what it is we love to do. The body still wants to play and move! I would literally finish coaching my kids and then walk the 500 meters to where the canoes were kept. It was fun. I paddled a regatta season, which was something new for me. We didn't have them in Australia. We only did sprints at Hamilton Island once a year. The regattas here are held every Sunday all through summer. It's a busy season.

In June 2007 Astrid was coming to visit. Each year she travels to Denmark to see her mother, my "Mormor" and she came through Hawaii on her way back to Australia. Astrid stayed with the family she used to work for at Diamond Head, the same house I went to for Tim's fortieth birthday five years prior! We travelled around the island sightseeing. She got to see my life here and joined in on some of my regular activities. We had a great time.

On one particular weekend she stayed in town at the Diamond Head house, and I went out to the North Shore to spend the night with my friend in Mokuleia. We had a lovely dinner and ended up talking story with another one of her friends who was teacher at Kuhuku High School.

Meanwhile Astrid was enjoying a dinner with her extended family and got to spend time and catch up with Christian (one of the boys she used to look after) obviously not a boy anymore!

He lives on the Big Island. From all reports, that was one interesting dinner. Nearly all the family that she used to take care of as kids were present.

There was much catching up of the years gone by and some of the family members for the first time were hearing about Astrid having a daughter and giving her up for adoption. It was an interesting tale for everyone to hear. Some of the family knew the story but because Christian lived on the Big Island, he wasn't up to date with the news of me finding her and especially the mutual connection through his family.

He was very intrigued and asked Astrid who the father was. For whatever reason he recognized the name but asked if the spelling was correct as he knew of a family with a very similar name. That was indeed the missing piece of the puzzle. It was one letter, one vowel which made all the difference. The spelling of his surname was incorrect, all the searching I did for that name was to no avail at the time. That's why I hit the dead ends and gave up seeking.

Everything happens for a reason, and he provided the momentum needed in the final stages of looking for the birthfather. With Astrid present, it could not have been more perfect, divine timing again. The dinner that night turned into solving the mystery of my birthfather and his whereabouts. There was a whole team working on it without me even knowing.

I knew instinctively that once the right person was told, who was in the know, the cards would tumble quickly, and they did! Christian was the link. He employed many people his company. He apparently made just a couple of phone calls and got all the information about my biological father he knew one of the daughters and everything opened up. It all fell into place. It was a Sunday and I was in Kailua paddling at the King Kamehameha Regatta and oblivious to all this happening the night before.

I hadn't raced yet and was getting some food. I stopped to talk story with Kamoa who was cooking huli huli chicken for the event. Kamoa is one of the Hawaiians I met initially at Hamilton Island. He would bring all the Hawaiian teams out to Australia each year, a great ambassador for the sport and a beautiful man.

He would often chant and do the blessing before the Canoe races. Just before I came to Hawaii he blessed one of my club Boats from Australia. Such a special being.

I always feel very comfortable around him, he has a real sense of calm and he's very connected with spirit. It would only be pertinent at this particular time that I am talking with him when Maggie comes over and said, "Hey Robyn, can I talk with you for a minute?" I could see in her eyes she had something very important to tell me. I excused myself and I felt Kamoa knew something was up.

I stepped aside with Maggie, and she said, "We have some news about your biological father." I was surprised and hanging on to the end of her sentence waiting for what she was to say next.

"I am so sorry to be the one to tell you this, we think we know who he is."

She went on to explain the course of events. One thing lead to another, a couple of phone calls and then double checking on the internet and newspaper articles. "Apparently there was an accident last year and he drowned."

I felt as if a lead balloon was dropped on me. I was in shock. I didn't know what to do, what to think, or anything.

She hugged me and kept apologizing to have to break that news to me, but really Maggie was the one to do it, she had been instrumental in including me in that family, making me feel part of it. I am grateful for her. She's an amazing person.

We parted for the time being, and I was just standing there, I guess I was tearful but they were inside tears. I felt a blank, a void and was trying to make sense of the information I just received. Kamoa turned to me with a look of understanding. From then on, all went quiet. I thought, "Oh my God, what on earth just happened?"

I needed to know the whole story, and hear what was what.

But I still had to paddle a race. I felt like I was skipping between dimensions, realities. Here is one timeline of I am about to paddle a race, and the other one of, your birth father who you have never met, is not alive anymore. "Bizarre" is the word at this time.

I had nothing really to say. I pulled myself back to game face and paddled, I didn't tell anyone, just did the job and left the beach and the canoes behind. I told Sarah that I had just found out some info on my birthfather and would explain later, but I couldn't stay. It was a blank drive back over the Pali to Diamond Head where Astrid was eagerly waiting.

Wow. This was what I wanted to know, and now it was all coming. I parked on the property and went in. Astrid greeted me with a hug and began to tell me what they discovered.

Christian knew one of my birthfather's daughters and had been talking with her on the phone. My biological father, had drowned after a heart attack whilst fishing at South Point on the

Big Island. It was all in the news and they went online to check that out.

Wow. What next? I was in a blur and not really sure on what I was feeling.

How are you supposed to feel when you find out who your biological father is and in the same breath you find out he died? It was the still point. If I could draw a description of the emotion I was feeling it would look like a circle.

There was no in between information or experience of the physical existence of this being for me. I had no memories, no story to draw feeling or emotion from. What I did have was something invisible, something inside me, part of me. He was a spark of light within my being. Strange to describe, and it is only now as I am editing this that I am having this awareness. I probably have always felt him, this energy is part of me, I just had never understood.

I rang Christian, he filled me in some more. He had been speaking with the eldest daughter and shared her number with me. She was expecting my call. This all happened so quickly. I am so happy that I was not doing this on my own and that Astrid was able to share this with me. It was just as intriguing for her.

Both of us decided to walk into Waikiki for some fresh air and to move some energy through the body. It was needed. Before the night was out, I had called the Big Island, spoke with the daughter, and she had invited us both to visit the following weekend to meet the family as they would all be gathering for Father's Day, to honor and celebrate their dad. Wow, everything was speeding up.

The flow was open. We stepped into it and the next thing you know, I am flying to the Big Island with my birthmother, her first time back since becoming pregnant with me, and we were about to meet my birthfather's ohana. Wow, careful what you ask for, you just may get it all!

CHAPTER 54

Big Island Roots

Christian and his family, who hosted us for the weekend were instrumental in making this second part of my reunion happen. Having him nearby was great. It was neutral territory for me. Astrid was probably having her own thoughts and feelings on what we were about to do. It was her first time back on the Big Island since she left nearly forty years ago.

All sorts of healing was happening on many levels.

Christian arranged for me to meet the eldest daughter at his house. Initially we met each other and spent some time alone. It was a fun and joyful meeting.

She is very down to earth, and couldn't believe it when saw me.

"You have Daddy's eyes," she said.

It was so great to connect with her. She shared some stories about her Father and then we joined the others in the main house. From the mountain above Kona, the sunset was a magical backdrop for this special gathering. I was in awe, overwhelmed by the magic I was experiencing.

Spirit is working through us and through the people around us in the most delightful and surprising ways. I feel very blessed.

The next day was like a mental day off, no talk or thinking about what we had just experienced. It was a fun day, remaining in the present and being active with the body. I was so happy to paddle a one man canoe that morning. It was exactly what I needed! We also swam with some turtles and enjoyed relaxing on the beach.

Astrid met up with a long time friend who used to live with the family when she worked in Hilo. That was a lovely meeting for her, so there was much happening for everyone. We were all being taken care of so well. In the afternoon, Christian drove us over to the house in Hilo, and I saw where Astrid used to live and work looking after the family, she was reminiscing.

I was happy to have a break from the spotlight, so to speak. It had been overwhelming in a good way. It was a relief to slip into the background for a moment and have the energy focused elsewhere.

That evening the three of us went for a beautiful meal in town and then it was time to rest. Even though the coqui frog choir were in full force, sleep came quickly.

The next day we woke early to a beautiful Mauna Kea mountain in the distance and clear blue skies. Astrid and I took a stroll. It was lovely, and we had a play in the sea pools.

Christian bought down the plastic sit on top kayak. This time I was starting to feel the nerves about meeting the rest of the clan.

I paddled that boat and was heading straight out to sea. I really wanted to keep paddling believe it or not. It felt so good out there. I was nervous about the day ahead. I had the most beautiful honu swim under me, one of the biggest turtles I have ever seen. It was very comforting as they are always a good sign for me.

After a delicious hot breakfast courtesy of our host, we packed up ready to drive south to the gathering. Christian was a pillar of strength for me that weekend. Very grounded energy. I will be forever grateful for the way he made us feel, creating a safe and comfortable space, for the magic to unfold.

CHAPTER 55

The Party @ Punalu'u

I was about to enter the realm of my birthfather's family. There are many relatives, I knew there was going to be some attention on me.

I took some long, deep breaths before walking towards the party.

We first met with my new half sister and she welcomed us warmly and started the introductions to more sisters, more gorgeous kids, and then the waterworks started. The tears broke the dam wall when I met one of the two brothers. He immediately saw his Dad in my eyes. To see me was a bit of a surprise, we hugged like we'd never been apart. I knew him. By this point we were both crying. A reunion, a remembrance, a reconnection, something inside was validated and no words were required. A hug is such a powerful gesture.

I met my birthfather's brother and his partner, who Astrid had great conversation with. Everyone was so welcoming. The other brother, who was not present interestingly enough, had been principal of the high school of the teacher I met in Mokuleia at my friends house just a week ago. She already knew him well before I did. So the night before I found out about my birthfather, I was already in conversation with someone who worked with my Hawaiian brother. Six degrees of separation. It blows my mind how things are woven and connected. The divine tapestry of life.

I met that brother and his family a year later in Honolulu. They were visiting from Utah. We had much in common with our teaching and love of sport, such a natural meeting and connection.

I feel so blessed for this.

I was fortunate to also meet a few of my birthfather's friends who used to play music with him.

I heard many endearing stories and received 'snippets' of his life through the eyes, the words and feelings of others that day. It was a full experience and I was exhausted, yet happy.

It was definitely time for me to get in the ocean. I could not wait any longer.

After the party, we drove a little ways and stopped at another beach. I was so happy to get wet and move in the water. I splashed, I swam, and then lay on my back, floating weightlessly for a few minutes. It was a divine moment. Fully supported, nurtured, connected, one with the water.

What a day. It was some five years after I started the search for my roots. This particular afternoon was the culmination of that process.

I am truly grateful for this healing, for this completion of the puzzle. It was important for me to know where I came from and to acknowledge this, the cultures, the lineage, the ancestors and to honor and bless it all. We are such complex beings yet innately simple and profound.

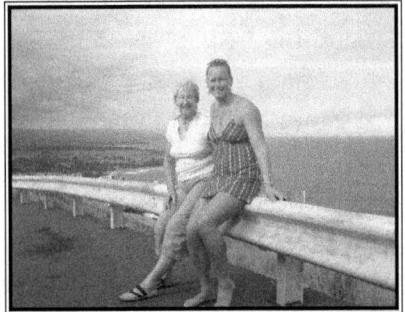

Since meeting the family, I have been welcomed to many gatherings and have attended when possible. I got to see a video of my birthfather's birthday celebration, the last one before his passing. I have a photo of a photo of him. We have some similarities. I have his blue eyes.

I definitely have his love for the ocean and nature, by the sounds of things. I have roots here in Hawaii. I love that the canoe brought me home.

CHAPTER 56

A little bird told me...

The very next morning after the party, I was back at the Ala Wai, coaching the kids. It was the heat of summer, a little later in the morning as they were on vacation. They were busy getting boats out and preparing for the practice.

I was sitting on a chair in the halau, quite focused and writing something. I looked up from my paper and a white pigeon, a dove, was at my feet. It was in no hurry to move. I instinctively reached down and put the edge of my hand up to its feet. Without any hesitation, the bird hopped on to the back of my hand. It was very tame, so I put it on my knee while I sat there. The kids came back from the dock and saw the bird sitting happily on my leg and were intrigued. I got them to take a picture and told them it was time to get the boats on the water for the session. I sat for a little longer on my own with the bird still on my knee, and suddenly I felt this incredible wave of calm come over me. I sat still and in so much peace, I was completely present with this being.

After a little while, I put the bird on my hand again, got up from the chair and walked the distance to the dock, Probably about 50 feet away. The beautiful white bird did not budge. I sat down on the dock this time by the water so I could see the kids. Again, I sat and stayed present and still. I knew this was something special, and if I may be bold enough to say, it was my birthfather's spirit coming through this bird. It was a message for me.

I felt he was happy that I had found and met his family, and through this bird he was able to convey the message so I could receive it. The words are just part of a message.

It is through feeling that we can receive
the essence of something.
If we tune in and be quiet enough to hear,
To observe,
We allow spirit, we allow God
To communicate to us through
Different channels in our every day existence.
Whether it is through an animal, or a soft
breeze, messages are all around us.

IN SUMMARY...

If I was to sum up the story I have just shared, then it's really about paddling.
The canoe was the vehicle that brought me back home on a multitude of levels.
People ask me now that I live here, what brought me to Hawaii? My answers range from "its my spiritual home, I have biological roots here, I was called by God and this is where I feel most connected, or I can keep it simple depending on who I am talking to, and say I came here to paddle."

What a loaded gift that has been and continues to be! I have helped many people get on the water for the first time or get them back after a long time away. We never know the depth of a simple action, what it will bring or the impact it will have on the individual's life.
When we paddle, we feel.

Wow. I am finally at the end of this book that I set out to write, such a long time ago. I knew it was the time to put it down, there was nothing else to do really other than this. When spirit guides, we listen and prioritize, for it always has our best interest at hand. It is my hope that this story inspires. It is also an entertaining vacation read whilst you lay relaxing on the beach here in Hawaii.

As I type, the rain outside is coming down and blessing me, blessing this process and blessing all the people that have been part of this particular adventure of mine, this dream. I paddled myself home, back to my roots, back to Hawaii, to my SELF, my source, to spirit.
With great love I thank you all.

You know who you are, and every one of you is an important part on this journey.
Y(our) timing, Y(our)placing, Y(our) potency
Mahalo Ke Akua

The writing of this story was a healing process for me. My intention in writing was to free up space in the mind for the new. I honor the journey, and I honor the people on the journey. They have been my divine reflections along the path and I am sincerely grateful.

We are God, spirit, having a human experience. Our stories are vast and numerous and we share without attachment, and we remember that we are not just our experiences. We all have a story, and that is what makes the life expression here on earth so interesting. Through our story, we can bring the magic of spirit into awareness by using our story to consciously awaken.

We are forever creating new experiences and new fresh ways of being that bring even more joy to this life. The time is now. We never get it done, it never ends. We enjoy our life, and endeavor to make it our highest and best expression yet. And so it is...

My body, my heart, my soul
The land, the ocean all part of me
A fusion of cultures and lineages
At my core, at my soul,
I AM One

Paddling Photos credit - Sue Neil Photography

"Paddling Home" - A Journey Back to Self

A personal story of Synchronicity, Healing and Reconnection...

"Outrigger Canoeing was not just a competitive sport for me,
It was an ancient and cultural remembrance, a feeling of
Oneness, and the chosen vehicle that would transport me back
to biological roots, my spiritual home and more importantly an
awareness and awakening to my higher self."